E OF 3-D CIVIL WA

UNKNOWN UNTI

IL WAR PHOTOGI

ES SOME OF THE

STEREOSCOPIC VIEWS

THE
CIVIL WAR
IN DEPTH
VOLUME II

ELL IN BATTLE

THE
CIVIL WAR
IN DEPTH
VOLUME II

HISTORY IN 3-D

BY BOB ZELLER

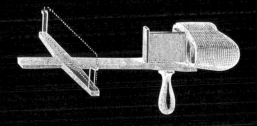

CHRONICLE BOOKS
SAN FRANCISCO

ACKNOWLEDGMENTS

As with the first volume of *The Civil War in Depth,* my ability to present the wide range of fresh and interesting images in this book is due to the private collectors listed on the picture credits page. In many cases, particularly with Robin Stanford, private collectors own views that do not exist in any public collections and therefore are otherwise unavailable. Because of their generosity, I am able to feature in this volume some of the choicest views from the best private collections in existence.

George S. Whiteley IV, dealer, photographer, archivist, and collector extraordinaire, again played a crucial role in the production of this volume. George was responsible for most of the color and black-and-white photography. It was gratifying to know that someone so steeped in the history and preservation of photographic antiquities was handling the original stereo views.

William A. Frassanito, the dean of Civil War photohistorians, and writer, historian, and reenactor Brian C. Pohanka took time from their busy schedules to review the manuscript. They offered many valuable suggestions. I am honored to call them friends.

Special thanks to Harvey Teal, the leading expert on early South Carolina photography, for his insights and detective work on the Osborn and Durbec plantation photos and for arranging a fact-finding mission to Rockville in the low country. Mary Panzer, curator of photographs at the Smithsonian National Portrait Gallery and authority on M. B. Brady, opened the door to the Meserve Collection. Noel G. Harrison and John Hennessy of the National Park Service at Fredericksburg provided the lost Cyclorama views as well as information about them and the Wilderness photos. Gil Barrett and Robert Krick, Jr., deserve special mention for providing last-minute information. Thanks to literary agent Sally McMillan, who represented both volumes. And a special nod to Bill LeBlond, senior editor of Chronicle Books, as well as Sarah Putman, Alan Rapp, and Jeremy G. Stout, who saw the potential in this idea and helped mold these books into what they are.

Thanks also to Paul Hogroian, Mary Ison, Eva D. Shade, and Stephen Ostrow at the Library of Congress; the Virginia Historical Society; Chris Hoolihan at the University of Rochester Medical School's Miner Library; John Dennis, editor of the National Stereoscopic Association's *Stereo World*; Brooks Johnson of the Chrysler Museum in Norfolk, Virginia; and Alison Devine Nordstrom at the Southeast Museum of Photography in Daytona Beach, Florida.

I also wish to thank Michael Ach, Sal Alberti, Ted Alexander, Harris Andrews, Wm. B. Becker, Al Benson, John Beshears, Sue Boardman, Mike Brackin, David Bull, Columbia (S.C.) Photo, Michael Congdon, Paul Crumlish, James Curtin, Dalmatian Black and White Custom Lab of Greensboro, N.C., Raymond Davenport, Norman Delaney, Michael D'Orso, Joe Ewers, Fields of Glory, Rob Gibson, Bryan and Page Ginns, Nicholas and Marilyn Graver, David L. Hack, Thomas Harris, Rod Hoffner, The Horse Soldier, Rick Houston, Matthew R. Isenburg, Ed Italo, Lawrence T. Jones, Larry Kasperek, Ross Kelbaugh, Lee Kennett, Jeffrey Kraus, Ron Labbe, the late Wendell B. Lang, Jr., Robert Liska, Tim McIntyre, Herb Milikien, Genevieve and Tom Morgan, Lloyd Ostendorf, John Pannick of Sword and Saber, Carl Parsons, Harry Roach, Len Rosa of War Between the States Memorabilia, Bob Ross, Brandt Rowles, John Saddy, Keith Snyder, David Starkman and Susan Pinsky at Reel 3-D Enterprises, Bruce Stocking, John Waldsmith, John Weiler, George Werner, James M. Zimmer, and Dave Zullo.

As always, I am blessed with the unqualified support of my wife, Ann; our children, Sara and Jesse; and the family historian, my mother, Ruth Walker Zeller.

This book is dedicated to Robin Stanford. So much of what is close to her heart fills these pages.

Library of Congress Cataloging-in-Publication Data available.

ISBN 0-8118-2524-8

Printed in Hong Kong.

Designed by Jeremy G. Stout

Distributed in Canada by Raincoast Books
8680 Cambie Street
Vancouver, British Columbia V6P 6M9

10 9 8 7 6 5 4 3 2 1

Chronicle Books
85 Second Street
San Francisco, California 94105

www.chroniclebooks.com

PICTURE CREDITS

TABLE *of* CONTENTS

ANTHONY'S INSTANTANEOUS VIEWS.
No. 430.
FOURTH OF JULY IN AND ABOUT NEW YORK.

A Company of Infantry marching through Chambers St., July 4th, 1860.

Published by E. Anthony, 501 Broadway, New-York.

No.

FROM
OSBORN & DURBEC'S
Southern Stereoscopic & Photographic
DEPOT,
223 KING STREET,
(Sign of the Big Camera,)
CHARLESTON, S. C.

EXCELSIOR.

GARDNER'S

PHOTOGRAPHIC ART

GALLERY,

INTELLIGENCER BUILDING,

511 Seventh Street,

WASHINGTON.

The Largest and Most Complete

ESTABLISHMENT

IN THE COUNTRY.

Gibson Brothers, printers, Wash.

[OVER.]

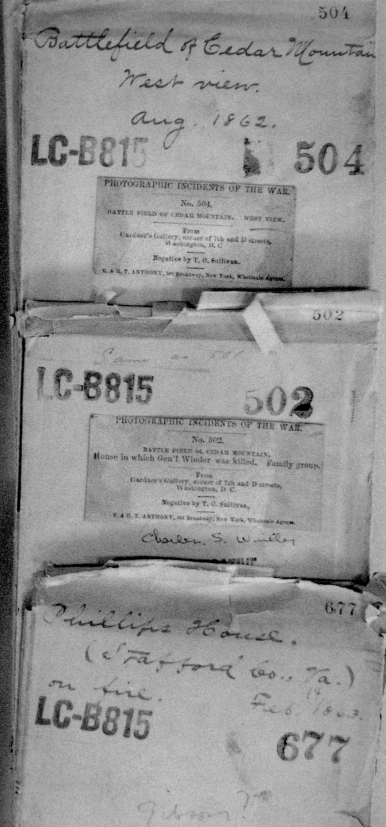

FOREWORD

GLASS PLATE NEGATIVES FROM THE LIBRARY OF CONGRESS IN THEIR PAPER SLEEVES

FOREWORD

THE CIVIL WAR IN DEPTH, PUBLISHED IN 1997, WAS

DESIGNED TO STAND ON ITS OWN

AS A ONE-VOLUME, 3-D PHOTOGRAPHIC HISTORY OF THE CIVIL WAR,

DEPICTING THE CONFLICT FROM BEGINNING TO END.

✳

There were no plans for a sequel,
even though some outstanding wartime stereo views were not included in that book.

Following the book's publication, however, I learned of Robin Stanford. A grandmother, history buff, and lifelong Texan from Houston, Stanford has spent the past thirty years quietly amassing a monumental collection of 3-D Civil War photos. To my knowledge, hers is the largest single collection of Civil War stereo views in existence.

In all, Stanford owns more than 1,500 views. The scope of the collection is staggering. She owns about 400 of the estimated 1,000 wartime stereo views produced by Alexander Gardner and his associates. She owns 700 to 800 of the more than 1,400 wartime stereo views issued by the E. & H.T. Anthony Company. She has the largest known group of original Osborn and Durbec Confederate stereo views of Fort Sumter and

the Charleston area. And she owns a group of rare stereo views of the Wilderness battlefield that photohistorian William A. Frassanito calls the "Rosetta Stone" of that series.

The collections of Civil War negatives and prints in the Library of Congress and the National Archives, as well as the Military Order of the Loyal Legion of the United States (MOLLUS) collection of prints at the U.S. Army Military History Institute, are far larger than Stanford's. But the vast majority of those negatives and prints are two-dimensional, half-stereo images. The negatives were originally stereo. But at some point, probably after the war, many of the original stereo glass plate negatives were separated, which in effect created two negatives of the same scene. Once cut, the two negatives often went

their separate ways. That all but eliminated the ability to make a stereo view. The separated negatives still serve the purpose of providing photographic prints of war scenes, which are often plenty dramatic in two dimensions. But in most cases, only one half of the original stereo negative or print still exists in the large government collections. So to see the photographs in 3-D, one must find original wartime stereo cards.

That is why Stanford's collection is so important. It is the most comprehensive record of 3-D images of the Civil War in existence. For many photos, she has the *only* extant examples in their original 3-D format.

Stanford has been interested in history since childhood. She minored in the subject at the University of Texas. She is married to

John Stanford, MD, a retired general practitioner and fellow lifelong Houstonian. At home in the late 1950s and early 1960s with their three small children, Robin spent many hours reading Civil War history. She did not begin collecting stereo views until about 1971. "I went to a small antique show and happened to notice this stereo viewer and some views," she says. "I was intrigued by it and I thought, 'This would be kind of fun to put in the living room of our farmhouse to use on rainy days.' We had a farm with an old farmhouse over in Giddings, east of Austin."

She developed more than a passing interest in stereo views: "I realized that you could see so much more in those views because of the three-dimensional qualities. You just seemed to step into scenes. And it fascinated me to see another time and place filled with people who were just as alive as I was—people who are all gone now. It was just like stepping into a time machine."

Stanford soon learned that her two passionate historical interests—the Civil War and Texas—were well-documented in stereo views. She began to focus on collecting these views. "I remember being surprised that so much of our history was so immediate," she says.

Today, a good original war view seldom sells for less than $100. But in the 1970s, they went for $20 or $10 or even less. Stanford often bought large lots of views. When the National Stereoscopic Association reprinted a wartime copy of the E. & H.T. Anthony Company stereo view catalog containing its "War for the Union" series, she began using it as a checklist. It was an ambitious endeavor. The catalog lists more than 1,400 war views. The numbering system starts at 2,282 and continues, with gaps, past 4,000.

But Stanford set about finding them, one by one. "At some point, I think I did make a conscious decision that I'd like to have as complete a stereoscopic record of the Civil War as possible," she says. "And when I would get new views, I would go to the catalog and check off the numbers."

Soon, she was collecting war views more avidly than her two sons were collecting baseball cards. As the years passed, one box grew to two, then three, then five, and then seven.

A SOUTHERN MYSTERY IMAGE

One of the most intriguing images in the Robin Stanford collection is this one, published here for the first time in any format. It was part of a series taken by the Confederate photographers Osborn and Durbec at Mt. Pleasant, just outside Charleston, most likely in 1860. A large gathering of Southern males, young and old, black and white, most dressed in fine clothes, have gathered on the bridge to Sullivan's Island. One man is posed in the act of spear fishing. Beyond that, the story behind the photo remains a mystery.

Presently, she has eight large plastic storage boxes full of Civil War views. Her Anthony collection, carefully arranged by number, fills three boxes alone.

In December 1998, Stanford graciously invited me to her home to see the collection. I knew from my own years of collecting and study that new photographic treasures of the Civil War continue to surface quite frequently. So I suspected that anyone who had collected for as long and relentlessly as she had was bound to own a treasure trove.

My suspicion was correct. As I slowly went through box after box of views, I found myself staring at unfamiliar images. Then I began seeing *series* of views I had never seen before, such as the Wilderness group. Stanford was gratified by my awestruck reaction. She believed she had many rarities, but hadn't really known for sure.

With the exception of three or four views, Stanford's collection has remained an untapped resource until now. Sixty-three of the 139 stereo views in *The Civil War in*

These advertisements from the *Harper's Weekly* newspaper show how extensively war photographs were produced and marketed. The ad on the left is from 1862. The one on the right was published in 1865.

Good News for the Army.

Hereafter we will send, *post-paid*, any of our PHOTOGRAPHIC ALBUMS ordered by soldiers for themselves or friends, giving an Album of the full value of the money sent.

Our Albums have the reputation of being *superior to all others in beauty and durability*, and range in price from 50 cts. to $50.

Our catalogue of

CARD PHOTOGRAPHS

now embraces about 5000 officers, army and navy, statesmen, actors, copies of works of art, &c. Catalogue sent on receipt of stamp.

Stereoscopes and Stereoscopic Views.

Our assortment of these is very extensive, including a great variety of views of the present war.

Catalogue sent on receipt of stamp.

E. & H. T. ANTHONY & CO,
501 Broadway, New York.
Manufacturers of Photographic Materials.

E. & H. T. ANTHONY & CO.,
Manufacturers of Photographic Materials.
WHOLESALE AND RETAIL
501 BROADWAY, N. Y.

In addition to our main business of PHOTOGRAPHIC MATERIALS, we are Headquarters for the following, viz:

STEREOSCOPES & STEREOSCOPIC VIEWS,

Of these we have an immense assortment, including War Scenes, American and Foreign Cities and Landscapes, Groups, Statuary etc., etc. Also, Revolving Stereoscopes, for public or private exhibition. Our Catalogue will be sent to any address on receipt of Stamp.

PHOTOGRAPHIC ALBUMS,

We were the first to introduce these into the United States, and we manufacture immense quantities in great variety, ranging in price from 50 cents to $50 each. Our ALBUMS have the reputation of being superior in beauty and durability to any others. They will be sent by mail, FREE, on receipt of price.

☞ FINE ALBUMS MADE TO ORDER.

CARD PHOTOGRAPHS.

Our Catalogue now embraces over FIVE THOUSAND different subjects (to which additions are continually being made) of Portraits of Eminent Americans, etc., viz: about
100 Major-Generals,   100 Lieut.-Colonels, 550 Statesmen,
200 Brig.-Generals,   250 Other Officers,   130 Divines
275 Colonels   75 Navy Officers,   125 Authors,
40 Artists.   125 Stage,   50 Prominent Women,
          3,000 Copies of Works of Art.
including reproductions of the most celebrated Engravings, Paintings, Statues, etc. Catalogues sent on receipt of Stamp. An order for One Dozen PICTURES from our Catalogue will be filled on the receipt of $1.80, and sent by mail, FREE.

Photographers and others ordering goods C. O. D. will please remit twenty-five per cent. of the amount with their order.

☞ The prices and quality of our goods cannot fail to satisfy.

Soldiers' Pocket Albums for 18 Pictures, 75 cents. 24 Pictures, $1 00.

Depth, Volume II are hers, and it is a privilege to use them. If this volume passes the test as an important new record of Civil War photography, it is a testament to her collection.

Other private collectors have made tremendous contributions as well. Among them, Mike Griffith has contributed several rare and outstanding views, as he did in the first volume. John Richter has made some wonderful finds in the past three years, several of which are reproduced here. Tony Chibbaro, in his first year of collecting, made some exciting Confederate discoveries. Steve Folio has generously allowed the reproduction of his stunning stereoscopic ambrotype of a Confederate artillery officer. Chet Urban's portrait of Custer is unforgettable. John Hennessy has graciously allowed the use of his series of views of the lost Cyclorama of Second Bull Run.

New finds have been numerous enough since the publication of the first volume to warrant a section called "Discoveries." In addition, this second work features a chapter of wartime 3-D images of African-Americans for the first time. Scattered throughout the book, as well as gracing their own chapter, are reproductions of fresh contact prints made from the original, 135-year-old glass plate negatives in the Library of Congress.

Finally, *The Civil War in Depth, Volume II* presents for the first time another little-known aspect of Civil War photography: Perhaps the most dramatic of all Civil War photos are 3-D views in color. Although color photography did not exist during the war, some views were hand-colored so carefully and exquisitely, they closely resemble color photographs. A generous selection of the best is presented here.

So step back into the nineteenth century once again through the magic of 3-D photography and see 139 of the greatest photographs of the Civil War, the way they were originally created and the way they were meant to be seen.

These are some of 658 original, intact glass plate stereoscopic negatives listed in the collection of the Library of Congress. They are still stored in paper sleeves with original wartime labels. The original negatives passed through a number of owners before being rescued by the library—for the price of the unpaid storage bill—from the basement of a warehouse in Hartford, Connecticut, in 1943.

**ORIGINAL GLASS
PLATE NEGATIVES**

THE LOST CYCLORAMA

A section of the lost Cyclorama of Second Bull Run.

DISCOVERIES

MUCH OF THE WORK OF THE LEADING CIVIL WAR PHOTOGRAPHERS IS WELL DOCUMENTED. **BUT NOT ALL OF IT.** TODAY, AT THE BEGINNING OF THE TWENTY-FIRST CENTURY, UNKNOWN CIVIL WAR PHOTOGRAPHS ARE STILL SURFACING.

IN 1997, FOR INSTANCE, THE FIRST TWO KNOWN IMAGES OF THE CSS *ALABAMA (other than those taken on deck)* CAME TO LIGHT.

New wartime stereo views are being found as well. Tony Chibbaro, a dentist from Prosperity, South Carolina, made a major discovery only months after beginning his collection of South Carolina views in 1998. Chibbaro found the first known nineteenth-century stereo view of Charleston photographer George S. Cook's famous combat action photograph at Fort Sumter.

The view is part of a rare and intriguing 1880 series called "Charleston and Vicinity During the War." These twenty or more images feature Cook's greatest wartime photographs. The series may have been issued by Cook's son, who took over his father's Charleston gallery in 1880 when the elder Cook moved to Richmond. Four views from the series are published in this volume.

In February 1995, Noel Harrison, historian at Fredericksburg National Military Park,

paid $5 at a Charlottesville, Virginia, thrift shop for a stereo view that showed an unfamiliar painting of the battle of Second Bull Run. He soon determined that the view showed a section of the lost Cyclorama of the Second Battle of Bull Run that had never been seen by modern historians. Last year, Harrison found three more views of the Cyclorama, including one showing another unknown section of the painting. All four views are featured here.

In 1998, while scouting for images at the National Portrait Gallery, I discovered that both halves of the stereoscopic negative still existed of one of the most important of M. B. Brady's Gettysburg photographs. The image shows the McPherson Farm with Brady himself in the picture. This was among the 5,200 negatives at the Portrait Gallery from the collection of the late Frederick Hill Meserve,

one of the first great collectors of war photographs.

But I was unaware of the true extent of my discovery until New Hampshire antiques dealer Robert Liska purchased an original Anthony view of the same scene on the eBay Internet auction site in early 1999. After reviewing William A. Frassanito's *Early Photography at Gettysburg*, Liska determined that his stereo view, and my discovery of both halves of the negative, documented for the first time that the original 3-D versions of this historic image still existed.

These and other recent discoveries of unknown 3-D war photos give us exciting new visual perspectives of the most dramatic period of our history. And they let us know, too, that more remains to be discovered.

DRAMATIC NEW IMAGES

**FIRST LOOK AT A
SLAVE CHURCH**

This view of the church for slaves on a plantation at Rockville, South Carolina, is published here for the first time. It was taken by Charleston photographers Osborn and Durbec, probably in 1860, and was part of their plantation series. Although some of the photographs from the series are known and published, these views from Robin Stanford's collection establish for the first time where most or all of the images were taken.

After a studious examination of the information written on the backs of the views, South Carolina photohistorian Harvey Teal was able to deduce that they were most likely bought by a British seaman aboard the HMS *Petrel,* which anchored in Charleston Harbor in 1862. The seaman apparently purchased the views as souvenirs and in February 1862 visited the places depicted in the photographs.

FROM THE OLD SOUTH

Osborn and Durbec boldly took their stereo camera inside the church, overcame the problems posed by low light, and made a remarkable photograph of a service in progress. Children crowd in front of the altar, while other parishioners sit on simple wooden benches. This print establishes for the first time that the image was taken on the "Rockville plantation." Rockville, South Carolina, is on St. John's Island, near the coast about 22 miles southwest of Charleston. Through additional research, Teal has determined that the church probably was Zion Chapel, an Episcopal church built for slaves in 1858 near Rockville. The Rev. Paul Gervais Jenkins was pastor.

INSIDE THE CHURCH

FAITHFUL SERVANTS

This view, another unpublished gem from the Osborn and Durbec plantation series, shows the graves of slaves who were so highly valued, they received their own engraved tombstones. The late "Janero" was faithful "to seven successive masters." In the back, the small tombstone is etched with what appears to be an elongated, African-style head—a trademark of black gravestones in the South Carolina low country.

THE SLAVE QUARTERS

Osborn and Durbec aimed their camera at the slave quarters and took a stereoscopic photograph looking up the long path in front of the slave homes, probably at the Rockville plantation. Although a similar image has been reproduced, this is apparently the first time this photograph has been published.

The only two negatives depicting M. B. Brady in the Meserve Collection at the National Portrait Gallery are these—the left and right stereo images of Brady (right) looking at the McPherson Farm buildings on the Gettysburg battlefield. The photograph has already been published as a two-dimensional image on the cover of *Smithsonian* magazine. But the fact that it still existed in its original 3-D format was not established until 1998.

This view of the bodies of South Carolina soldiers laid out for burial was the last of the "lost" Gardner death studies known to have been taken at Gettysburg. A half-stereo, two-dimensional print surfaced in 1994 and was first published in *Early Photography at Gettysburg* by William A. Frassanito, who said it "was among the rarest of the rare." This view from the Robin Stanford collection is the only known 3-D version and is published here for the first time.

Entered according to Act of Congress, in the year 1863, by Alex. Gardner, in the Clerk's Office of the District Court of the District of Columbia.

7. Two monitors and Old Ironsides firing on Sumter.

THE FIRST COMBAT STEREO PHOTOGRAPH

The 3-D version of Cook's famous action scene of three Union gunboats (the vessels are nearly invisible) firing on Fort Moultrie and Fort Sumter was first published in *The Civil War in Depth*. It was a makeshift view that I created from the two very similar photographs of the scene that Cook took using his single-lens camera. Although the *Mobile Advertiser* reported in 1863 that Cook intended to "reduce these pictures to stereo-scopic dimensions," no commercially produced stereo view of the scene was known to exist until 1998, when Tony Chibbaro found this 1880 view.

This outstanding view of Union soldiers poised at right shoulder shift while on the march is another rare, unpublished gem from the Stanford collection. The back reads: No. 17–"Return of a foraging party near Columbus, Kentucky." It was sold by Carbutt's Garden City Photographic Art Gallery in Chicago. Perhaps more of this series will someday surface.

A NEW IMAGE OF A CLASSIC SCENE

Although labeled "Gen. Grant and Staff," this remarkable view is actually a rare and notable Indian wars view by William Illingworth. It shows U. S. Grant's son, Fred, in camp with Seventh Cavalry officers during Gen. George A. Custer's Black Hills Expedition of 1873, according to the book *Prelude to Glory*. This drinking party undoubtedly occurred while Custer, who shunned drinking, was away from camp. Although Custer said no drinking or card playing occurred while he was away, a 1927 memoir by expedition member William R. Wood said Fred Grant "was drunk nearly all the time." Among the officers shown, 2nd Lt. Benjamin Hodgson (seated at left) was killed at Little Big Horn and Capt. Frederick Benteen (seated fifth from left with the cocked hat) was blamed for not coming to Custer's aid. This image, probably a private photo, somehow came to be mass produced—and mislabeled—by the International Stereoscopic View Company, probably in the mid-1870s.

A SPURIOUS VIEW OF GRANT DRINKING IN CAMP

New York City, U. S. A.

International Stereoscopic View Co.

Gen. Grant and Staff, 226.

THE LOST

The *Cyclorama of the Battle of Second Bull Run* was one of the largest paintings ever made. It was 50 feet tall and 400 feet long. Fifteen artists under the direction of French painter Theophile Poilpot took two years to paint it. When it went on display in Washington, D.C., in 1886, "it instantly became a major attraction," writes historian John Hennessy. By 1910 it was apparently in storage. And what happened to it after that is unknown. The best surviving depiction of it may be these four stereo views issued in the late 1880s by J. F. Jarvis of Washington, D.C. Historian Noel G. Harrison recently uncov-

CYCLORAMA

ered all four views. The two views on page 22 show sections of the painting that had never been seen by modern historians until Harrison's discovery. The view at the bottom of page 23, which shows the climactic Union assault on the unfinished railroad cut on the afternoon of August 30, 1862, reveals much detail not visible in other reproductions of this part of the painting. The views do have some 3-D effect because a set was built in front of the painting that included trees and fencing. More than thirty Civil War cycloramas were painted in the late 1800s. Nearly all are lost.

CHAPTER ONE

TAKING IT EASY

Unidentified Union officers enjoy the pleasures of camp in this drinking
image, which may have been privately produced by Alexander Gardner.

CAMP LIFE

On *April 15, 1861,*

THE DAY AFTER FORT SUMTER SURRENDERED TO THE CONFEDERATES, **PRESIDENT ABRAHAM LINCOLN DECLARED** *by* PROCLAMATION THAT

AN INSURRECTION EXISTED.

HE CALLED FOR 75,000 VOLUNTEERS.

Militia and volunteer units from New York, Pennsylvania, Massachusetts, and other states began rushing toward Washington, which was still largely unprotected against attack. One of the first units to respond, the 6th Massachusetts, was attacked by Rebel sympathizers in Baltimore before bivouacking in the chamber of the U.S. Senate.

As the troops poured into the capital, camps sprouted and photographers began appearing with their cameras. Most of the photography consisted of custom-made portraits on metal or glass plates that soldiers purchased for themselves or their families.

But several photographers also began making stereo views for commercial sale to the general public. The best known is a series called "Camp Scenes" taken mostly in 1861

for the E. & H.T. Anthony Company. By the end of the war, the company's catalog listed eighty-three views in this series, although the category was also used for some miscellaneous war views, including a number of photographs of Harper's Ferry and several of Morris Island, South Carolina.

Many of the views were taken at Camp Essex, an important bastion overlooking the B & O Railroad at Relay, Maryland, just outside Baltimore; or at Camp Cameron in the capital city itself. Although most of the men at these camps were on ninety-day enlistments, they still had the time to create elaborate cooking and living areas and establish a higher standard of living than seen in most army camps during the war.

Anthony's camp scenes apparently were

quite popular. They are still readily found in today's antique photo markets. And in 1869, they commanded a premium over most of Anthony's other views, even other war views. The catalog lists "War for the Union" views at $4 a dozen. Camp Scene views sold for $5.50 a dozen.

In May 1861, one enterprising Washington photographer, William H. Smith, began providing custom stereo views to soldiers at Camp Cameron. Smith, who advertised himself as a "stereoscopist," had a gallery at 482 H Street in Washington. He actually had a special backmark printed for views he took of members of the 7th Regiment of New York State Troops, the "National Guard." It included a place for the soldier to write his company and tent number.

☆

AMONG THE FIRST TO ANSWER THE CALL

These soldiers probably were part of the 8th Massachusetts Regiment, one of the first four regiments to answer the call in the spring of 1861 for troops to guard Washington. In this May 1861 photograph, they stand outside their tents at Camp Essex just south of Baltimore. The 8th Massachusetts was a three-month regiment and was mustered out of the service on August 1, 1861 without ever firing a shot in combat.

A COMMANDING VIEW

Here, some of the 8th Massachusetts soldiers pose next to their cooking area. The 8th Massachusetts was at Camp Essex from May 16 to July 29, 1861. The camp was on a hilltop that provided a commanding view of the surrounding Maryland countryside, including the all-important rail line between Baltimore and Annapolis and the Thomas Viaduct.

The 7th New York State Militia (National Guard) left New York City for Washington on April 19, 1861 after a special appeal from President Lincoln requesting troops to protect the ill-guarded capital. This rare image, probably published here for the first time, was part of a series made especially for the regiment during their one-month stay at Camp Cameron in May 1861. The 7th was *the* elite New York militia organization, with many Manhattan bluebloods in the ranks. Many went on to become officers in volunteer units. Like many militia units North and South, the 7th wore gray uniforms.

RELAXING AT CAMP CAMERON

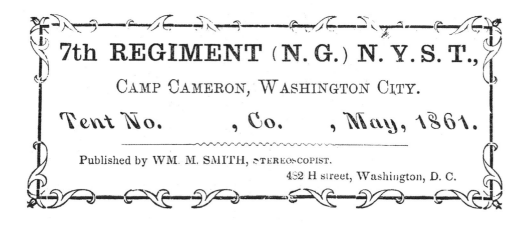

7th REGIMENT (N. G.) N. Y. S. T.,

CAMP CAMERON, WASHINGTON CITY.

Tent No.   , Co.   , May, 1861.

Published by WM. M. SMITH, STEREOSCOPIST.

452 H street, Washington, D. C.

~ (back mark) ~

PHOTOGRAPHER IN A TREE

Photographer James Gibson, working for M. B. Brady during the Peninsular Campaign, obviously was enthralled by the vast scope of the Army of the Potomac encampment on the Pamunkey River at Cumberland Landing, Virginia, in May 1862. He took at least fifteen photographs of the sprawling camp, including several panoramas and this unusual image taken from the upper branches of a tree.

AN ARMY IN TENTS

Photographer George Barnard, who worked for Brady early in the war, probably took this dramatic landscape photograph. It shows a camp, perhaps the camp of the 66th New York Volunteers, near the Chickahominy River in Virginia during the Peninsular Campaign in the spring of 1862.

THE WAR FOR THE UNION.

PHOTOGRAPHIC HISTORY.

This candid camp scene by photographer Alexander Gardner shows Lt. Col. Samuel Owen of the 3rd Pennsylvania Cavalry taking a nap in camp at Westover Landing, Virginia, in August 1862, following the Seven Days battles. This is reproduced from a fresh contact print made with the original glass plate stereoscopic negative.

Although the original caption for this image says it shows pickets cooking their rations near Fredericksburg, Virginia, on December 9, 1862, photohistorian William A. Frassanito notes that there is far too much foliage for December. Frassanito believes it may be a "lost" image from an interesting series taken early in the war that includes a bogus "Dead on Matthews Hill" image showing four soldiers playing dead.

PHOTOGRAPHIC HISTORY.

THE WAR FOR THE UNION.

PLAYING CARDS

Nothing is certain about this photograph other than it shows two soldiers playing cards in front of their winter quarters.

There is no label on the back, only the penciled notation: "Scene in Camp."

WAR AT THE BEACH

This Anthony Company stereo view, probably made in 1861, is entitled simply, "Camp Life." It was part of the company's "Camp Scenes" series. We do not know where it was taken or

who is in the picture, but it may be the only Civil War beach-bathing scene ever photographed.

This striking image, reproduced from a new contact print off the original glass plate negative in the Library of Congress, shows two young military telegraph operators in camp outside Petersburg, Virginia, in August 1864. Timothy O'Sullivan, one of the finest photographers of the war, took the photograph.

Sutler W. G. Johnson poses outside his tent with the 2nd Division, 9th Army Corps, Army of the Potomac, near Petersburg, Virginia in November 1864. Sutlers were notoriously crooked. The caption on this view observed: " . . . with condensed milk at a dollar per can . . . [a soldier's pay of] thirteen dollars a month did not prove sufficient to keep a fellow in cash more than one or two days per month."

1861 The War For the Union. 1864

1861 Photographic War History. 1865

2448.   A Sutler's Tent.
[FOR DESCRIPTION OF THIS VIEW SEE THE OTHER SIDE OF THIS CARD.]

A DEFENDER OF THE UNION

An unidentified black sergeant is shown in this ninth-plate
tintype portrait by an anonymous photographer.

THE AFRICAN-AMERICAN
EXPERIENCE

AFRICAN-AMERICANS APPEAR IN HUNDREDS OF CIVIL WAR–ERA STEREO VIEWS,
BOTH BEFORE AND AFTER THE EMANCIPATION PROCLAMATION WENT INTO EFFECT IN 1863.
PLANTATION SCENES WERE A STAPLE FOR SOUTHERN PHOTOGRAPHERS.
OSBORN AND DURBEC APPARENTLY PRODUCED

the first series of
PLANTATION STEREO VIEWS

with the images they took around Charleston
and at a plantation at Rockville, South Carolina, most likely in 1860.

During the war, fugitive slaves, known as "contraband," flocked to the Union armies. Many became servants, exchanging one form of servitude for another that included a small wage. They were frequently photographed in Union Army group shots and camp scenes.

In 1862, Congress authorized the recruitment of black soldiers. Some of the first began to see action on June 7, 1863, at Milliken's Bend, Louisiana, where Confederates attacked a Federal garrison that was manned in part by the African Brigade. There, black soldiers proved they could and would fight.

As black regiments were formed, they were photographed just as white regiments

were. And in 1864 and 1865, black soldiers in uniform began appearing regularly in the views produced by the E. & H.T. Anthony Company. They were depicted in their various wartime roles as teamsters, cooks, laborers, and soldiers. These views form an important photographic record of black service in the war.

The army's statistics show that 178,975 blacks enlisted in the Union Army. More than 38,000 lost their lives. For many male slaves fleeing the South, joining the Army was the best opportunity immediately at hand.

Despite the many stereo views of African-American soldiers, blacks were later depicted in stereotypical roles or made the subject of

derisive humor in views produced during the golden age of the stereograph, which included the latter part of the nineteenth century and the first two decades of the twentieth century.

Even Alexander Gardner, the great war photographer, cast the servant "John Henry" in a stereotypical light in an essay that accompanied one camp scene photo in his famous *Photographic Sketchbook of the War:* "A legend was current at headquarters that J. H. had been discovered hanging by his heels to a persimmon tree. It is needless to say that this was a libel, originating in a scurrilous picture of that African, drawn by a special artist."

SLAVERY WITHOUT THE HARSHNESS

Some photographs of slaves cast them in settings that belied the harshness of their lives. This image, number twelve in Osborn and Durbec's historic 1860 plantation series, shows "old Bacchus fishing from the bridge" at the planter's summer residence on the "Rockville plantation."

OUTSIDE THE SLAVE PEN

This is a Brady & Co. view of the Price, Birch & Co. slave dealership in Alexandria, Virginia. The establishment was nicknamed the "slave pen" by photographers because of the prison-like accommodations for the human merchandise. The photographer's wagon sits in front of the building, which was, in fact, used as a prison for errant Union soldiers during the war.

As fugitive slaves by the thousands flocked to safety behind Union lines, officers hired young blacks, even children, as servants, perpetuating a system of subjugation. This 1861 stereograph was taken at the camp of Lt. John Shaw, 2nd Rhode Island Infantry, Army of the Potomac, in Washington, D.C. Shaw (right), as captain, was killed at Spotsylvania on May 12, 1864.

SERVING THE ARMY

The church played a major role in African-American life during the nineteenth century, before and after slavery was abolished. This view, taken by Brady & Co. in Richmond probably on Easter Sunday in April 1865, shows the congregation of the First African Church outside their place of worship on Broad Street. The church was erected in 1802 and had one of the largest black congregations in the South.

THE FIRST AFRICAN CHURCH

GUARDING THE ORDNANCE

Here, an African-American soldier in an overcoat stands guard at shoulder arms next to a new 12-pound brass cannon on the ordnance wharf at City Point, Virginia, late in the war. This was No. 2382 in the Anthony Company's "War Views" series.

THE 26TH COLORED REGIMENT

The 26th United States Colored Infantry, pictured here in columns of companies, went into action outside Beaufort, South Carolina, at Honey Hill, also called Grahamville, on November 30, 1864. The regiment was part of an unsuccessful assault against Georgia militia in an effort to enlarge the Union-held territory and to cut the Charleston and Savannah Railroad.

On the evening of July 18, 1863, the 600 men of the 54th Massachusetts Colored Infantry marched down the beach shown in the top image and led a massive Union assault on Fort Wagner located on the beach of Morris Island just south of Charleston Harbor. The attack was repelled. The regiment suffered losses exceeding 40 percent, including its commander and organizer, Col. Robert Gould Shaw. But the battle again proved that black soldiers were combat-worthy. These images, by photographer Sam Cooley, show the outside and inside of the fort after it was abandoned by the Confederates in September 1863. The story of the 54th Massachusetts is told in the movie *Glory* (1989).

**THE ASSAULT OF
THE 54TH
MASSACHUSETTS**

ASSISTANCE FOR FREED SLAVES

The 3-D effect is vivid in these two stereographs taken in Beaufort, South Carolina, which was occupied by the Union Army in November 1861. The federal government created the Freedmen's Bureau to aid freed slaves. Idealistic teachers and workers from New England went south to help. The top image shows a school and store for freedmen, while the bottom image shows the Beaufort library, which was apparently converted into a hospital.

REPRESENTATIVES

Although the opportunity was short-lived, some blacks took seats in Southern state legislatures during Reconstruction. This is an early postwar image of the North Carolina House of Representatives, including several black members, posed outside the state capitol in Raleigh. Charlotte photographer Rufus Morgan published the stereo view.

BLACKS IN POWER

LINN'S LOOKOUT

Hundreds of Union soldiers had their photographs taken on Lookout Mountain in Chattanooga, Tennessee. This quarter-plate tintype, most likely made by Royan Linn, a Lookout Mountain photographer, shows Lt. Wilmon W. Blackmar (pointing) of Co. H, First West Virginia Cavalry, and a colleague.

PORTRAITS

While outdoor scenes numbered in the thousands,

SOLDIER PORTRAITS

UNDOUBTEDLY TOTALED IN THE MILLIONS.

During the first half of the war, most soldiers had their portraits taken as a cased image known as a tintype or ambrotype. The tintype image was made on a thin piece of iron, while the ambrotype was on a small piece of glass. The metal or glass was coated with a sticky solution called collodion that was made sensitive to light. The metal or glass thus became the photograph itself. It usually was sealed behind a brass or gilded mat and a piece of glass, then placed inside a small, hinged case.

The carte de visite was another form of portrait photography that was popular during the Civil War. These card photographs were slightly smaller than today's sports trading cards and were their forerunners. There were no sports stars in the mid-nineteenth century, but many family albums of carte de visite photographs also included the

images of famous generals, statesmen, actors, or actresses.

When photography was introduced in 1839, people thought it was the end of painting. Photographs captured the portrait far more accurately than paintings, so who needed paintings anymore? Paintings and drawings survived, of course, but photography has remained the primary method of portraiture since its invention.

One of the finest collections of Civil War–era portraits is the Meserve Collection, which is now part of the Smithsonian Institution's National Portrait Gallery. The Meserve Collection includes more than 5,200 glass plate negatives for cartes de visite. Among the subjects are dozens of wartime generals and statesmen. The collection also includes hundreds of negatives of midgets, giants and giantesses, and other

P. T. Barnum performers.

The collection was assembled by Fredcrick Hill Meserve, who became enthralled with Civil War photography in 1897 when he was thirty-one, after he bought a bundle of old photographs for $1.10. The bundle included exquisite prints by Mathew Brady. Meserve's collection eventually included the negatives of some of the most important photographs of Abraham Lincoln.

The two Meserve Collection portraits reproduced in this chapter are from glass plate negatives exposed in a four-lens camera. The four-lens camera produced two pairs of side-by-side negatives. Although not designed as a stereoscopic camera, the four-lens camera nonetheless produced two pairs of images that work in 3-D.

☆

THE NATIONAL

ULYSSES S. GRANT

On one of his visits to Washington, D.C., during the war, Lt. Gen. Ulysses S. Grant stopped by Brady's gallery on Pennsylvania Avenue to have this portrait made with a multiple-lens camera.

This is from a fresh print of two of the negatives in the Meserve Collection.

PORTRAIT GALLERY

Although rich with Union generals and officers, the Meserve Collection has few Confederates. An exception is this multiple-lens portrait of the Confederate Gen. James Longstreet in civilian clothes taken at the Brady studio shortly after the war. Longstreet lived until 1904, outlasting most of his contemporaries of high rank.

JAMES LONGSTREET

A TOUGH GENERAL AND HIS COMMANDERS

This Brady & Co. stereo view—one of the finest group portraits of the war—shows Gen. Winfield Scott Hancock, commander of the Second Corps, Army of the Potomac, with his division commanders at Cold Harbor, Virginia, in June 1864. Standing from left to right are Francis C. Barlow, David B. Birney, and John Gibbon. Hancock, Barlow, and Gibbon were wounded at Gettysburg.

A STEELY-EYED VETERAN

At age sixty-five, Brig. Gen. Edwin V. Sumner was the oldest battlefield corps commander of the Union Army when this photograph was taken in 1862. A Mexican War veteran, Sumner directed his corps in their ill-fated attacks into the West Woods at Antietam and up Marye's Heights at Fredericksburg. He died of illness in 1863 before he could take a new command in the Department of the Missouri.

111. Group at Paint Rock — Gen'l Braxton Bragg.

Although he suffered repeated failures and defeats in the western theater of the war, Confederate Gen. Braxton Bragg still maintained an imposing posture in this early postwar photograph in the mountains of his native North Carolina.

Photographer Rufus Morgan, who also issued the image of the North Carolina House of Representatives, published this obscure image.

A REBEL WHO LOST

After the war was over, Maj. Gen. Edward O. C. Ord, a twice-wounded Union corps commander, posed with his wife and daughter for the camera of M. B. Brady at the Confederate

White House in Richmond. Behind them is the table upon which Robert E. Lee signed the surrender of the Army of Northern Virginia.

A MILITARY FAMILY

Entered according to Act of Congress in the year 1865, by E. & H.T. Anthony & Co. in the Clerk's Office of the District Court of the U.S. for the So. District of New York.

A SPY AND HIS TRUSTED MOUNT

Secret Service operative John C. Babcock posed for Alexander Gardner's camera near Antietam in October 1862 with his horse "Gimlet." Almost fifty years after the war, Babcock told the editors of the *Photographic History of the Civil War* that no small part of his success at scouting and spying had been due to "Gimlet," which he rode throughout the war.

GENERAL INGALLS'S DOG

Dogs have been in front of the camera since photography started. It was no different during the Civil War, where one canine image was marketed by the E. & H.T. Anthony Company. This is the Dalmatian of Gen. Rufus Ingalls, the quartermaster of the Union Army. The photograph was taken in Virginia in 1865.

Newspapers could not reproduce photos during the Civil War, only drawings and maps. One of the most prolific of the "special artists" who followed the armies was Alfred R. Waud of *Harper's Weekly*. Waud was good friends with Alexander Gardner, whose assistant, Timothy O'Sullivan, took this picture in Devil's Den at Gettysburg less than a week after the battle. Waud's sketches were turned into woodcut engravings so they could be reproduced in the paper.

Pauline Cushman's effectiveness as a Union spy is debated, but there is no dispute that she lived a tumultuous life. Captured after passing information gained from her relationships with Confederate officers, Cushman was sentenced to die but was rescued by Union forces. Years later, a forgotten figure, she became addicted to drugs and committed suicide.

American & Foreign   Portrait Gallery.

CORPORAL ALEXANDER WILLIAMS

The eyes were slightly retouched in the right-hand image of Cpl. Alexander Williams of the 9th New York Cavalry, making these two cartes de visite appear to be different. But these are two exposures of the same moment from a multiple lens camera. Williams is shown here in Albany, New York in November 1861, two months after he enlisted. He survived his three-year term and was mustered out in October 1864.

THE COMMON INFANTRYMAN

Little is known about this classic field portrait of a common Union soldier. He may have been from Rhode Island or Michigan, because companion images show regimental field bands from those states. He may have been in a militia unit, since his uniform appears to be gray. The photographer is unknown, but the print was made around the turn of the century from an original negative that was already losing emulsion.

This stereo photograph of Gen. George Armstrong Custer and his dog in camp was probably taken in 1864. The card has survived for more than 130 years in near-mint condition. It is particularly important as a photographic record because the Library of Congress index says no negative exists for this photograph.

CUSTER

CHAPTER FOUR

THE INTERIOR OF A CIVIL WAR–ERA PHOTO STUDIO

THE CIVIL WAR IN COLOR

COLOR PHOTOGRAPHY DID NOT EXIST DURING THE CIVIL WAR, BUT THAT DID NOT STOP PHOTOGRAPHERS FROM PUTTING COLOR IN THEIR PICTURES.

THEY HIRED **TINTING ARTISTS** WHO HAND PAINTED THEM.

The results varied from awful to magnificent. The best specimens show Civil War photography in an exciting new light. The existence of 3-D Civil War photographs in color has been relatively unknown until now, except among collectors and Civil War photography experts. This chapter reproduces some of the finest known examples.

The tinting done by the E. & H.T. Anthony Company was generally superior to that done at Alexander Gardner's gallery. Gardner's hand-tinted views tended to be too thickly painted—the most common problem with hand-tinted commercial views. One original Gardner hand-tinted Gettysburg view in my collection is so thickly painted, it completely obscures the 3-D image of Little Round Top.

The Anthony Company had some outstanding tinters. They had a delicate touch, and knew that the smallest amount of diluted watercolor went a long way.

"You build up the color gradually," says Brandt Rowles, a stereo view collector who has experimented with hand tinting and lectured about it at National Stereoscopic Association conventions. "You have to be careful not to apply too much paint or it will look ghastly. Sometimes you have to wonder whether people played with painting views at home. Because when you see some of these views, you say, 'Who would have bought that? It looks horrible.' "

Hand-tinted war views were among the most expensive views in the 1868 catalog of the E. & H.T. Anthony Company. They cost $6 a dozen, while non-tinted war views were $4.50 a dozen. Most other views in the catalog were priced at $2.50 to $3 a dozen.

The prices suggest that war views were popular enough to command a premium over other images, even several years after the war. But interest was fading as the decade ended. In the 1869 catalog, war views had dropped to $4 a dozen, $5 a dozen if colored. And in the 1870 catalog, the price of non-tinted views was down to $3.50 a dozen.

Hand-tinted Civil War photographs have been rarely published in 2-D and almost never in 3-D until now.

**THE LAST JULY 4
BEFORE THE WAR**

Patriotic fervor was growing in the North as New York state militia units paraded in New York City on July 4, 1860, the last Independence Day before the war. The Anthony company took a number of instantaneous views of the parade; the two reproduced here were also carefully hand-colored. In the top view, the instantaneous camera (see page 87) stops the action as an infantry regiment marches down Chambers Street. Below, the 79th New York, or Cameron Highlanders, regiment, dressed in their kilts with bagpipes playing, march in Tryon Row.

This mint-condition view, entitled "Writing to Friends," is one of the finest surviving examples of a hand-tinted wartime stereograph. Owned by Maryland collector Gil Barrett, the view was taken at Camp Essex outside Baltimore in 1861 and published in the Anthony "Camp Scenes" series. The letter writers appear to be sitting in church pews. The tinting is particularly effective because the artist did not color the entire photograph.

WRITING TO FRIENDS

THE FAIRFAX COURT HOUSE

Union troops advancing toward Bull Run skirmished with the Rebels on July 17, 1861 near Fairfax Court House, shown here. Then they settled in for the night before moving deeper into Virginia. The backmark on this early Anthony war view purports that it was taken "just after the Grand Army passed to fight the Battle of Bull Run" on July 21.

BRIDGE OVER THE CHICKAHOMINY RIVER

The engineers of the 15th New York Volunteers built this temporary bridge over a part of the Chickahominy River during the Peninsular Campaign in 1862. Known as Woodbury's Bridge, it was one of the many makeshift bridges in the swamplands around the river that gave the Union Army the ability to move and allowed it to reinforce embattled regiments in the battles of Fair Oaks and Gaines' Mill.

Entered according to the Act of Congress. in the year 1862, by Gardner & Gibson, in the Clerk's Office of the District Court of the District of Columbia.

Entered according to Act of Congress, in the year 186_ by Alex. Gardner, the Cle____

Entered according to Act of Congress, in the year 1863, by Alex. Gardner, in the Clerk's Office of the District Court of the District of Columbia.

Whether they were Union or Confederate, the fallen soldiers in Alexander Gardner's dramatic Gettysburg stereo views usually ended up in blue uniforms if the views were tinted. The top view is the stereoscopic variant of Gardner's famous large-plate image called "Harvest of Death." It shows dead Union soldiers who fell during the second day's battle. As photohistorian William A. Frassanito has observed, their bodies are without shoes, indicating they were behind Confederate lines at some point and were relieved of the needed footwear. The bottom view shows Confederate dead in the Slaughter Pen, an area located along Plum Run at the base of Big Round Top a few hundred feet southeast of Devil's Den.

THE DEAD OF GETTYSBURG

THE JAMES RIVER

By 1865, the Union controlled the James River in Virginia from Norfolk to Hopewell. The river became a primary means of moving men and materiel from the coast to the battlefronts around Petersburg. The top view shows troop transports on the James. The double-turreted monitor USS *Onandaga* appears to be anchored in the background. The bottom view shows the river at City Point, Virginia, and the drop-off spot for troops and supplies.

This view of "Cincinnati," the war-horse of Lt. Gen. Ulysses S. Grant in 1864 and 1865, was taken at City Point, Virginia. Grant received the thoroughbred during a visit to St. Louis in January 1864. Miller's *Photographic History of the Civil War* quotes Grant as saying that Lincoln "was a fine horseman and rode my horse 'Cincinnati' every day" while visiting City Point in 1865.

A HORSE THAT LINCOLN RODE

His middle name came from the legendary American Indian warrior. He himself was one of the most aggressive U.S. Army warriors. Sherman is best known today for his march through Georgia as well as the phrase, "War is hell." This wartime view was part of the Anthony Company's "Prominent Portraits" series.

WILLIAM TECUMSEH SHERMAN

FORT BRADY

Members of Company C, 1st Connecticut Heavy Artillery, pose with their guns at Fort Brady on the James River in March 1865. These guns dueled with Confederate land batteries and warships for several months in late 1864 and early 1865. The fort is now part of the Richmond National Battlefield Park and the ramparts still exist in remarkably good shape.

BREASTWORKS NEAR THE APPOMATTOX RIVER

Soldiers on both sides dug miles of trenches and breastworks in Bermuda Hundred, Virginia, between Richmond and Petersburg, during 1864 and early 1865. Evidence of many of those trenches and defensive works still remains today. This view shows a section of federal works near the Appomattox River.

PHOTOGRAPHIC HISTORY

THE WAR FOR THE UNION.

BOONDOGGLE

The Dutch Gap Canal project undoubtedly was the most photographed military boondoggle of the Civil War. More than two dozen images were taken of this ultimately useless effort to build a canal that would bypass a Rebel stronghold at a loop in the James River. Soldiers nicknamed the profile created by the left bank at the far end of the canal "Jeff Davis."

THE DUTCH GAP CANAL

HOOD'S HEADQUARTERS IN ATLANTA

From this home in Atlanta, Confederate Gen. John Bell Hood directed the doomed defense of the city in the summer of 1864. George Barnard took this view after Sherman's federal troops occupied the city on September 2, 1864.

CHAMBERSBURG AFTER THE FIRE

Gen. Jubal Early's Rebel cavalry rode into Chambersburg, Pennsylvania, on July 30, 1864 and threatened to burn the city unless the citizens paid $500,000 in currency or $100,000 in gold to help make up for Union destruction in the Shenandoah Valley. The citizens could not raise the money, so Chambersburg was burned. Here are the remains of the Lambert and Huber Straw Board Mill.

New York photographer George Stacy took a series of views at Fort Monroe in Virginia, including this hand-tinted view of Camp Hamilton. The vital fort, located at Hampton Roads where the James River meets the Chesapeake Bay, remained in Union hands throughout the war. This 1861 view shows the camp of the 5th New York Zouaves.

CAMP HAMILTON

From the parapet of Fort Sumter, reduced to rubble after four years of bombardment, Union officers gazed toward Charleston as boats clustered in its harbor. It was April 14, 1865. That day, the Union flag was raised in victory inside Fort Sumter. That night, President Lincoln was assassinated at Ford's Theater.

A FATEFUL DAY AT A BATTERED FORT

PHOTOGRAPHIC HISTORY

THE WAR FOR THE UNION.

Entered according to Act of Congress in the year 1865, by E. & H.T. Anthony & Co. in the Clerk's Office of the District Court of the U.S. for the So. District of New York.

2621. La rivière du Potomac,
Etats-Unis Amérique.

THE RAREST FORMS OF

A GLASS TRANSPARENCY

This is a reproduction of a glass stereo view, which may be the rarest form of commercial Civil War stereo photography. The transparent glass views allowed images to be seen with brilliant backlighting, thus providing unmatched clarity, detail, and 3-D definition. But glass views were fragile, more cumbersome than card views, and prohibitively expensive. They cost $24 a dozen in 1869, compared to $4 a dozen for card views of the war. This French-issue Anthony view shows not the Potomac River, but the Appomattox River and a hospital ship wharf at City Point, Virginia.

CIVIL WAR STEREOGRAPHS

First Lt. Columbus W. Motes, a Confederate artillery officer from Athens, Georgia, left his photograph gallery on April 24, 1861 to go to war. He was wounded in the left hip and right shoulder at Sharpsburg. He fought courageously at Gettysburg. Somehow, Motes survived and resumed his photography career when the war ended, working in Athens until the turn of the century. This full-sized stereoscopic portrait of Motes is reproduced from an ambrotype. It is the only known stereoscopic cased image of a Rebel soldier. The small reproduction shows the full Mascher stereoscopic case, complete with fold-up viewer.

A STEREOSCOPIC AMBROTYPE OF A REBEL

A REGAL-LOOKING OFFICER

This half-plate, hand-tinted ambrotype shows Capt. James A. Holeman of Company A of the "Roxboro Grays," the 24th North Carolina Regiment of the Army of Northern Virginia. Holeman (1832–1905) served all four years of the war. He was wounded at Drewry's Bluff in 1864 and captured at Five Forks on April 1, 1865.

CONFEDERATES

COMMERCIAL STEREO PHOTOGRAPHY
WAS SELDOM DONE IN THE SOUTH DURING THE WAR.
BY FAR THE MOST PROLIFIC PRODUCERS WERE
CHARLESTON PHOTOGRAPHERS OSBORN AND DURBEC,
WHO WERE MOST ACTIVE IN 1860 AND 1861,

AND GEORGE S. COOK, THE ONLY SOUTHERN PHOTOGRAPHER TO MAKE AND SELL STEREOGRAPHS THROUGHOUT THE WAR.

Original Osborn and Durbec views are distinctive because of their bright orange card mounts and small backmarks (only found on some views) that advertise their Southern Stereoscopic and Photographic Depot at 223 King Street under the "Sign of the Big Camera."

Osborn and Durbec produced several small series of views showing scenes of Fort Moultrie, Fort Sumter, and Morris Island a few days after the Confederates took over Sumter in April 1861. But South Carolina photohistorian Harvey S. Teal can find no evidence of their working past 1861. By the time Cook took his famous combat action photographs inside Fort Sumter in September 1863, he had an assistant identified as James Osborn—probably Durbec's former partner.

The best of Cook's wartime work was featured in a distinctive series of at least twenty stereographs issued in 1880 called "Charleston And Vicinity During the War." Some of the best examples are featured in this chapter and elsewhere in this book. The series may well have been produced and sold by Cook's son, George L. G. Cook, who opened his own gallery in Charleston in 1880 after his father moved to Richmond.

George S. Cook managed to stay in business throughout the war in part because he invested in blockade runners, which brought him photographic equipment and supplies as well as a tidy profit. In his private account book, Cook recorded 10 percent dividends from "Cobia stock . . . China D . . . (and) Enslows Schooners," according to author Jack C. Ramsay, Jr., Cook's great grandson, in his book *Photographer . . . Under Fire.* The

Cobia and *China D* were successful blockade runners, while "schooners" referred to vessels owned by J. A. Enslow.

In 1863, the *American Journal of Photography* reported that there had been "very little photography in Jeffdom for the past two years," but noted that Cook was still working "by favor of our British cousins who run the blockade . . ."

Cook moved from Charleston to Columbia, South Carolina, in 1864, but his new studio was burned when the city fell to Sherman. Cook sold photographs of the 1865 flag-raising ceremony at Fort Sumter. It is possible he purchased another photographer's negatives, but the images seem to reflect his own distinctive style.

20. Interior of Institute or Secssion Hall 1860. Showing figures of fashionable people 20 years ago.

SECESSION HALL

On December 20, 1860, South Carolina formally seceded from the Union in a ceremony in this large room inside the South Carolina Institute Hall. The building immediately became known as Secession Hall. But it was destroyed by a fire that swept through Charleston on December 11, 1861. This view is part of the "Charleston and Vicinity During the War" series of George S. Cook photographs. The series can be dated to 1880 from the information in the caption.

A SLICE OF "GONE WITH THE WIND"

A sense of Southern plantation life before the war oozes from this image. But when photographer E. W. Sinclair took this view of the Smith Plantation near Beaufort, South Carolina, in 1862 or 1863, the area had already been occupied by Union troops.

With that Southern flair for style, the men of the Charleston artillery militia pose with their brass cannon at the Battery in this view by Osborn and Durbec. The date is unknown, but the image probably was taken in 1861, well before the harsh realities of war hit the port city.

Undeterred by poor lighting, Osborn and Durbec took their stereo camera inside the Rebel "Iron Clad Battery" floating off Morris Island to make one of the most interesting photographs of the first conflict of the Civil War. From within this iron-sheathed barge, fiery secessionist Charles Ruffin launched one of the first shots at Fort Sumter, firing one of these two Columbiads (or perhaps one of two other unseen cannon). The young Confederate in the foreground is unidentified.

14. Confederate Picket Camp. Occupation of the soldiers, Reading,

GUARDING THE WATERWAYS

Cook took this stereograph of a Confederate picket camp at Stono Inlet, South Carolina, in 1861. In the foreground, handling the cooking chores, are three slaves—the personal servants of one or more of the Confederates in this picture.

AN ARTILLERY DRILL

Another 1861 stereograph by Cook shows a Confederate artillery unit sighting their field piece. The precise location is uncertain, although the Valentine Museum identifies it as Fort Sumter. This is one of the guns of the Palmetto Battery, a light artillery militia unit.

13. Confederate Artillery working a field piece.   Sighting.

On May 2, 1863, Confederate Gen. Thomas J. "Stonewall" Jackson was mortally wounded by his own troops at this spot along the Plank Road as he returned to his lines during the battle of Chancellorsville. This obscure view, made around 1880, was uncovered by collector John Richter in 1997. The small, granite memorial still exists alongside a newer, larger one.

There is no known stereo photograph of the Confederates' leading cavalry commander, J. E. B. Stuart. But there is this image of his relatively fresh grave. Stuart was mortally wounded on May 11, 1864 in a cavalry battle at Yellow Tavern outside Richmond. He died the next day in the Confederate capital and was laid to rest on this hillside at Hollywood Cemetery. This photograph probably was taken in 1865.

J. E. B. STUART'S GRAVE

1861 The War For the Union. 18   1 Photographic War History. 1865

3618. Grave of General J. E. B. Stuart.
[FOR DESCRIPTION OF THIS VIEW SEE THE OTHER SIDE OF THIS CARD.]

CHAPTER SIX

AN OCCUPIED CITY

This is the right panel of a three-plate panorama of Chattanooga,
Tennessee, probably taken by George Barnard in 1863 or 1864.

THE WEST

PHOTOGRAPHER GEORGE N. BARNARD,
WHO FOLLOWED SHERMAN THROUGH TENNESSEE, GEORGIA,
AND SOUTH CAROLINA IN **1864 and 1865,** MADE

THE MOST EXTENSIVE SERIES

of battlefield images taken in the western theater of the Civil War. Barnard started as a
daguerreotypist in his native New York in 1846. He spent

THE FIRST THREE YEARS OF THE WAR

taking photographs for M. B. Brady and Alexander Gardner. In **December 1863,** he
was hired by the Topographical Branch of the Department of Engineers, Army of the
Cumberland, and moved from New York to Nashville.

Barnard spent most of his time in Nashville making photographic copies of maps. The photographic reproduction of maps was one of the most significant ways photographers could help the army. And it gave photographers access to the top commanders. Barnard was fortunate that his commander, Captain of Engineers Orlando M. Poe, loved photography. Poe encouraged Barnard's field photography as well as his portrait work.

Author Keith Davis, in his outstanding book *George N. Barnard, Photographer of Sherman's Campaign,* says that most of the top Union commanders, encouraged by Poe,

visited Barnard's studio in Nashville. Poe obtained copies of their cartes de visite, then asked for autographs. He once mailed several to his wife, warning her to be careful with them because with the signatures they would be valuable.

Poe eventually donated his collection to his alma mater, West Point. Among the photographic treasures in his collection: the most complete known set of stereo views of the Wilderness battlefield photos featured later in this volume.

Other photographers besides Barnard did manage to capture a few memorable stereo

views in the West. The Library of Congress has half-stereo negatives for at least five photos taken in and around Vicksburg in February 1864 by the photographer William R. Pywell. The Baton Rouge photographers McPherson and Oliver took a memorable series of stereographs at Port Hudson, Louisiana, after the 1863 siege. And the view of the return of a Union foraging party near Columbus, Kentucky (reproduced in the Discoveries section), carries the number '17,' indicating the existence of a series of Kentucky views, most of which apparently remain to be uncovered.

☆

GALLERY POINT ON LOOKOUT MOUNTAIN

The most spectacular place for a photography studio in Chattanooga, Tennessee, was on top of Lookout Mountain. Photographer Royan M. Linn set up shop at his "Gallery Point Lookout" and took thousands of images of soldiers, officers, and generals. In the background, the Tennessee River winds past the city and the mountain.

PRISONERS OF WAR

Rebel soldiers who were captured in the battles of Missionary Ridge and Lookout Mountain were herded into the Knoxville Railroad Depot in Chattanooga, where they awaited a train that took them to the uncertainty and hardships of Northern prisoner of war camps.

THE WAR FOR THE UNION.

PHOTOGRAPHIC HISTORY.

2654

Union engineers built this impressive military bridge over the Tennessee River at Chattanooga in 1864. On the far side of the river is Cameron Hill. In the background looms Lookout Mountain.

On the top of Lookout Mountain, Lulu Falls seemed to make George N. Barnard briefly forget about the war. He became a travel photographer for the moment, capturing a scene of tranquillity with the same camera that recorded so many images of destruction.

A LAST REBEL STRONGHOLD

PORT HUDSON

The Confederate earthen fort on the Mississippi River at Port Hudson, Louisiana, disabled five of the seven vessels commanded by Adm. David Farragut when he attempted to run past it on March 14, 1863. It also withstood furious assaults by land on May 27 and June 14. When Vicksburg surrendered on July 4, Port Hudson became the Confederates' last stronghold on the Mississippi River. But the bastion surrendered only four days later. These two views were part of a series made by the Baton Rouge photographers McPherson and Oliver. The top view looks south toward the fort and the river. The bottom view shows the detritus of war within the earthworks after the Rebels surrendered.

View from the front of State House, Nashville, Tenn., during the battle of Dec. 1864, showing in the distance the Federal camps, in the foreground soldiers and civilians watching the fight.

Barnard took this scene in front of the statehouse in Nashville. The soldiers and civilians gathered on the prominence were said to be watching the battle of Nashville raging in the distance on December 14, 1864.

WATCHING A BATTLE

This is Chickasaw Bayou just north of Vicksburg, near where Gen. W. T. Sherman made a bloody and unsuccessful assault on December 29, 1862, attacking the left of the Confederate line defending the Mississippi River town. William R. Pywell took the stereograph in February 1864.

CHICKASAW BAYOU

Chickasaw Bayou, Mississippi

Entered according to Act of Congress, in the year 1862, by M. B. Brady, in the Clerk's Office of the District Court of the District of Columbia.

THE FORGOTTEN CONFLICT

**INDIANS AT THE
WHITE HOUSE**

On March 27, 1863, President Lincoln took a moment's respite from the war to meet Kiowa and Cheyenne leaders at the White House. Although Lincoln himself did not pose with the Indians for a photograph, this M. B. Brady view taken in the White House conservatory shows Mary Todd Lincoln standing at far right, while Lincoln's secretary, John G. Nicolay, stands at center. All four of the Indian leaders seated in front of them would be dead within twenty months. From left, War Bonnet and Standing in the Water were killed on November 29, 1864 in the Sand Creek massacre; Lean Bear was murdered by regular army soldiers as he peaceably approached them wearing the peace medal President Lincoln had given him; Yellow Wolf (at right) died of tuberculosis.

OTHER
DAY
ANPETU TOKECA

WHITNEY & ZIMMERMAN, PHOTOGRAPHERS.

SAINT PAUL, MINNESOTA.

No. 73. People Escaping from the Indian Massacre of 1862, in Minnesota, at Dinner on a Prairie. Photographed by one of the Party.

In August 1862, the Sioux Indian War erupted in Minnesota when angry Indians revolted in protest over the lack of food on their reservations. The short-lived rebellion cost perhaps 500 lives, mostly civilians. This view shows some of a party of sixty-two who were guided from the massacre area through the wilderness to safety by a christianized Indian named Anpetu Tokeca (Other Day). The photographer reportedly was a young Yankee who had arrived in the country a day before the massacre started, to make photographs of Indian life. He became one of the refugees.

AMERICAN REFUGEES

CHAPTER SEVEN

NAVAL OFFICERS

The officers of the USS *Philadelphia* pose on the deck of the ship
in Charleston Harbor at the end of the war.

THE NAVIES

⸺ • ⸺

THE CONTEST FOR SUPREMACY ON THE SEAS

DURING THE CIVIL WAR
WAS SPORADICALLY PHOTOGRAPHED.

SOME ASPECTS OF THE SEA WAR WERE WELL DOCUMENTED
by the camera, OTHERS WERE IGNORED.

THERE ARE PLENTY OF PHOTOGRAPHS OF THE USS *MONITOR,* NONE OF THE CSS *VIRGINIA (MERRIMACK).*

And the first known photographs showing the full length of the CSS *Alabama* did not surface until 1997.

The *Alabama*'s ill-fated battle with the USS *Kearsarge* off Cherbourg in France on June 19, 1864 provides the most tantalizing mystery of Civil War naval photography. Some 15,000 spectators watched the battle from other ships and from shore, among them Cherbourg photographer François Sebastien Rondin. Contemporary written accounts suggested Rondin had actually made a photograph of the most famous Civil War naval battle. Unfortunately, it is almost certainly untrue, according to Norman C. Delaney, Professor of History at Del Mar College and a longtime student of the battle. But there is fascinating evidence alleging that it did happen, Delaney revealed in *Military Images* magazine in 1998.

Frederick Milnes Edge, an Englishman who traveled to Cherbourg to investigate the battle for his government, said in a thirty-six-page report that Rondin had photographed the battle from "the summit of the old church tower" in the city. "I was only able to see the negative, but that was quite sufficient to show that the artist had obtained a very fine view indeed of the exciting contest," Edge wrote.

Austin Quinby, a marine corporal on the *Kearsarge,* wrote in his journal on June 30, 1864, that "Mr. Rondin a photographer is on bord [sic] taking views of the deck . . . He brot [sic] on bord Photographs of the fight which

are good . . . They are 7x9 a fine Picture showing the Alabama going down and the Kearsarge riding the waters in all her glory."

Delaney has uncovered a carte de visite of the battle sold by Rondin that shows the scene exactly as Quinby described it. Unfortunately, it is a drawing. Delaney believes Rondin indeed tried to make a photograph. "But the attempt did not succeed," Delaney reports. "The ships were six miles from shore, probably little more than specks wreathed in the smoke of battle." And if Rondin had actually made a photograph of the battle, he would have had no need to sell a drawing of it.

No. 103.

PENSACOLA STEAM FRIGATE, OFF ALEXANDRIA.

Entered according to Act of Congress, in the year 1865, by Alex. Gardner, in the Clerk's Office of the District Court of the District of Columbia.

THE *PENSACOLA* STEAM FRIGATE

The steam-powered sloop-of-war USS *Pensacola* marked the transition from the old Navy to the modern Navy in the Civil War. Steam power had replaced sails, although the sails were still at the ready. Ironclads were yet to come. The *Pensacola* is shown here at Alexandria, Virginia, in early 1861 after it steamed past Rebel guns and helped open the Potomac River below Washington.

THE FIRST SUBMARINES

The Confederate Navy was the first to successfully use submarines against enemy vessels. In this 1864 photograph by Charleston photographer George S. Cook, women and children, probably his family and friends, pose next to a David-class semi-submersible torpedo boat, the forerunner of the CSS *Hunley* submarine. Note the young man sticking his head out of the hatch.

In this new print from the original glass plate negative in the Library of Congress, Union naval officers examine the superficial damage suffered by the Union's first ironclad, the USS *Monitor*, in its epic battle with the CSS *Virginia* off Hampton Roads on March 9, 1862.

The USS *Passaic* was one of the monitors that battled with Confederate shore batteries in Charleston Harbor from 1863 until the end of the war. Here, off Port Royal, South Carolina, the men and officers gather on deck for a prayer service. E. W. Sinclair, working for photographer Sam Cooley, made the stereograph.

**DAHLGREN
AND HIS GUN**

In this Brady & Co. stereograph taken aboard the USS *Pawnee* in Charleston Harbor, Rear Adm. John A. B. Dahlgren stands before a Dahlgren gun, which he invented. Dahlgren was the commander of the South Atlantic Blockading Squadron and led Union naval operations in and around Charleston from 1863 to the end of the war.

**WATCHING FOR
BLOCKADE RUNNERS**

The cat-and-mouse game of running the Union blockade—and catching Rebel blockade runners—continued throughout the war, although by 1865 little was getting past Union ships. In this Anthony view, a Union officer aboard the USS *New Hampshire,* ready with his telescope, stands watch for blockade runners outside Charleston Harbor.

1868. STEAMER CHICORA—NOTED BLOCADE RUNNER

A FORMER BLOCKADE RUNNER

The steamer *Chicora* was a blockade runner during the war. Afterwards, the ship was modified and served on the Great Lakes, where this view was taken probably in the late 1860s or 1870s.

THE WRECK OF THE *COLT*

The loss of the blockade runner *Colt* off Sullivan's Island near Charleston may not have been the disaster this image suggests. If cornered by federal vessels, blockade runners often were purposely run aground on the Confederate-held coast. Their pursuers could not follow without suffering the same fate. The cargo, which could be easily salvaged, was worth far more than the ship.

Wreck of blockade-runner Colt, off Sullivan's Is

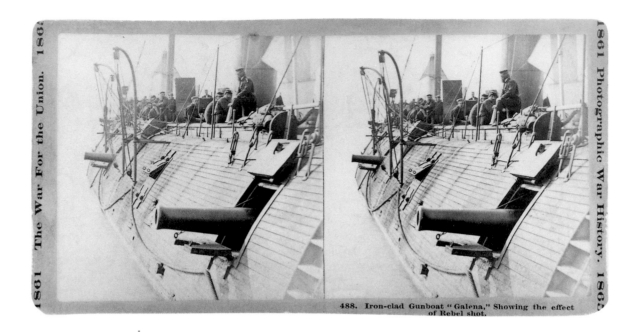

488. Iron-clad Gunboat "Galena," Showing the effect of Rebel shot.

AN EARLY IRONCLAD WARSHIP

The USS *Galena* was one of the first Union ironclad warships. But the iron that was used to plate her sides was not enough. In a duel with Confederate Fort Darling on the James River in July 1862, *Galena*'s armor was pierced by Rebel shells in several places, including one spot visible just above the end of the muzzle of the closest gun.

THE FATE OF THE TEASER

The CSS *Teaser* was a converted tugboat that held its own as a consort to the famous CSS *Virginia* during its battle with the USS *Monitor*. But by itself on July 4, 1862, the *Teaser* was no match in a fight with the *Monitor* and another warship on the James River. Her crew escaped to shore, but the damaged *Teaser* became a Union prize, complete with valuable dispatches.

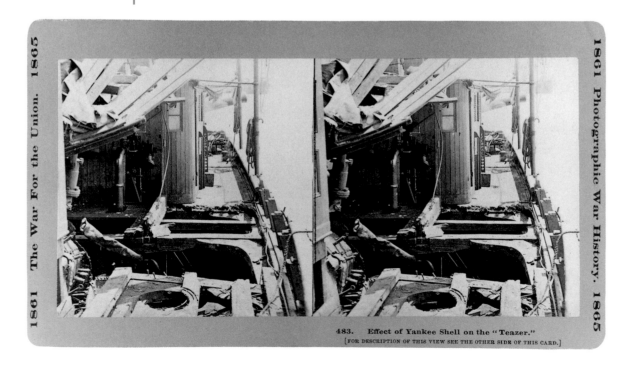

483.   Effect of Yankee Shell on the "Teazer."
[FOR DESCRIPTION OF THIS VIEW SEE THE OTHER SIDE OF THIS CARD.]

JOÃO F. CAMACHO
PHOTOG.
MADEIRA

Florida   St. Louis   Jolie Blockade runner

A TENSE STANDOFF

This original 1864 stereo photograph from Madeira Islands, displayed on a European mount and carrying the imprint of the Madeira photographer on the back, is one of the finest naval views of the Civil War in existence. Now in the collection of Robin Stanford, the view shows the CSS *Florida,* the USS *St. Louis,* and the blockade runner *India* at anchor off Funchal in late February 1864. The *Florida* was one of eight Rebel raiders that plundered Union commercial vessels during the war. It took thirty-seven ships before being captured in October 1864. In this view, the enemy ships warily coexist in the neutral harbor. The *St. Louis*'s captain had to unload his guns to prevent his patriotic crew from attacking, which would have caused a diplomatic debacle. The *Florida,* whose guns were under repair at the time, was not particularly welcome here, and steamed back out into the open sea on February 29 after obtaining a meager resupply of water, biscuits, and only twenty tons of coal from the Madeira port captain.

CHAPTER EIGHT

ATLANTA

Union troops under Gen. W. T. Sherman burn ties, heat rails, and twist them
in downtown Atlanta before their march to the sea in 1864.

CITIES AT WAR

THE CIVIL WAR RAVAGED

A NUMBER OF AMERICA'S CITIES, LARGE AND SMALL, AND HAD ITS IMPACT ON MANY OF THEM.

ATLANTA; RICHMOND; COLUMBIA, SOUTH CAROLINA; CHAMBERSBURG, PENNSYLVANIA:

ALL WERE **BURNED**. CHARLESTON WAS **BOMBARDED**. VICKSBURG WAS **BESIEGED**.
SHELLS FELL ON THE DOORSTEP OF WASHINGTON ITSELF IN 1864.
EVEN NEW YORK WAS **BATTERED** BY THE 1863 DRAFT **RIOTS**. THROUGH IT ALL,
THE HEARTBEAT OF THE HOME FRONT PULSED STRONGLY IN THE CITIES.

Some of the most fascinating wartime stereo views were taken in New York, the home of the E. & H.T. Anthony Company, the country's largest seller of stereo views, photographs, and photographic supplies. The Anthony Company was the Kodak of nineteenth-century America.

The photographs of the Union Square rally and the return of the 69th Regiment in 1861, as well as the tinted views of the July 4, 1860 parade, are examples of the Anthony Company's remarkable "instantaneous" photography. As early as July 4, 1859, almost two years before the war, the Anthonys were taking photographs that stopped action almost as effectively as a modern camera.

Many wartime cameras required expo- sures of at least four or five seconds or longer. If the lighting was poor, it might take twenty- five seconds. Blurred figures are so common in Civil War photos, most people assume all of them required long exposures.

But the Anthony Company began sell- ing "instantaneous views" starting with the city's 1859 Independence Day celebration. Some 1859 views stopped the movement on Broadway even on a rainy day.

"Anthony's Instantaneous Stereoscope Views are the latest photographic wonder," the company boasted in an 1860 advertise- ment. "They are taken in the *fortieth part of a second,* and everything, *no matter how rap- idly it may be moving,* is depicted as sharply and distinctly as if it had been perfectly at rest." To do this, the company developed the mechanical camera shutter and also found ways to improve the sensitivity of the light- sensitive collodion mixture poured on the glass plates, William and Estelle Marder write in their book *Anthony, The Man, The Company, The Cameras.*

While the instantaneous process was not widely used in Civil War field photography, some images seem instantaneous, such as the marching view on page fifty-two. And Miller's *Photographic History of the Civil War,* pub- lished in 1911, says Charleston photographer George S. Cook used the "instantaneous pho- tographic apparatus of the present day" to shoot his famous combat action photographs at Fort Sumter in 1863.

☆

THE GREAT UNION MEETING

On Saturday, April 20, 1861, six days after Union Maj. Robert Anderson surrendered Fort Sumter, thousands of New Yorkers rallied in Union Square to support the war. "Such a mighty uprising of the people has never before been witnessed in New York, nor throughout the whole length and breadth of the Union," wrote the *New York Herald.* Anderson, who sailed directly from Sumter to New York, was one of the speakers at the rally.

READING WAR BULLETINS

Passersby stopped outside the offices of the *New York Evening Post* to read handwritten bulletins about the war. The bulletins described some of the stories that appeared in the evening paper, which was available from the newsboy standing under the bulletin on the left.

NEW

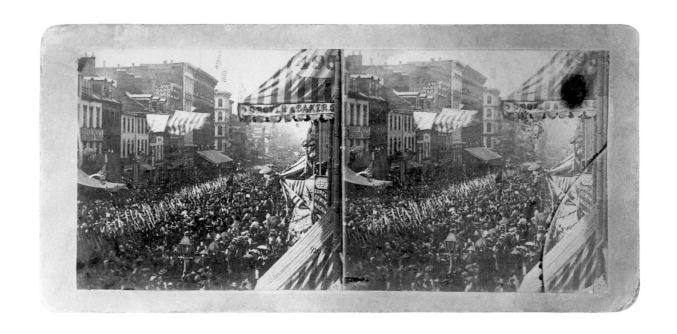

YORK CITY

After shedding blood in combat at Bull Run, the 69th New York State Militia returned to a triumphant welcome in New York City during the first week of August 1861. The regiment had left New York in a hurry on April 23—three days after the Great Union Meeting—to help protect Washington. After defending the capital city in May and June, it marched out to Manassas, Virginia, in July and fought at First Bull Run. One officer and forty-four enlisted men were killed or mortally wounded. In this rare Anthony instantaneous photograph that freezes the motion of a fluttering American flag, the crowds pack the street on a hot summer day to cheer the soldiers during their march up Broadway.

**THE RETURN OF
THE 69TH**

PHOTOGRAPHIC HISTORY

THE WAR FOR THE UNION.

THE FIRE ZOUAVES SAVE THE DAY

In early May 1861, a fire broke out in a tailor shop near the Willard Hotel in Washington. The dashing Col. Elmer Ellsworth and his "Fire Zouaves," who were mostly New York firemen, became heroes when they kept the fire from spreading. On May 24, Ellsworth became a Union martyr when he was shot to death after removing a Confederate flag from the Marshall House in Alexandria. This Brady & Co. view shows the gutted tailor shop. The Smithsonian Institution is in the distance.

ENCAMPMENT ON THE WHITE HOUSE GROUNDS

During the first months of the war, soldiers bivouacked in the U.S. Capitol building and camped on the grounds of the White House. In this view from an Anthony series of Washington, D.C., images, the soldiers' makeshift shelters crowd the lawn as the White House looms through the trees.

Encampment on the White House Grounds.

WASHINGTON

On July 11, 1864, Confederates under Jubal Early marched into the Maryland suburbs and began to threaten Washington itself. In Silver Spring, just across the Maryland line, they burned the home of Postmaster General Montgomery Blair. The ruins are shown here. The Rebels withdrew the next day without launching a serious attack.

In the aftermath of the assassination of President Lincoln, a photographer aimed his camera at the almost-finished U.S. Capitol building and took a photograph of it with black bunting on the columns. The construction yards are in the foreground.

PHILADELPHIA

A HAVEN FOR SOLDIERS

To care for Union soldiers passing through Philadelphia on their way south, the city's citizens created the Union Volunteer Refreshment Saloon at the foot of Washington Avenue. Operating strictly on contributions, the saloon served more than 750,000 meals during the war.

A WARTIME CELEBRATION

Although the war never reached San Francisco, Union troops were stationed there to guard against any Confederate efforts to capture the port and control the California gold fields. Many of the troops participated in this Independence Day ceremony at Washington Square in 1862.

SAN FRANCISCO

WATKINS' PACIFIC COAST, 22 and 26 Montgomery Street, opposite Lick House entrance, San Francisco.

Photographic Views of California, Oregon, and the Pacific Coast generally—embracing Yo Semite, Big Trees, Geysers, Mount Shasta, Mining, City, etc., etc. Views made to order in any part of the State or Coast.

Washington Square, July 4th, 1862, San Francisco.   321.

MONTGOMERY

On February 18, 1861, Jefferson Davis put his hand on this Bible and saw this view from the steps of the capitol building at Montgomery, Alabama, as he took the oath of office as the first president of the Confederate States of America. "Our present political position has been achieved in a manner unprecedented in the history of nations," he told the audience.

WHERE DAVIS WAS INAUGURATED

ATLANTA

WHITEHALL STREET

George N. Barnard took this view of Whitehall Street in downtown Atlanta just before Sherman left the city on his march to the sea. The roofs of the railroad cars in front of the Atlanta Hotel are crowded with Union soldiers. At right is the home of *The Intelligencer*, Atlanta's first successful newspaper and the only local paper to survive the war.

DESTROYING THE RAILROAD

Barnard's camera also captured soldiers heating and bending railroad rails to render them unusable. Sherman was determined to leave nothing useful behind when he departed the city, and he ordered it evacuated of all civilians. Sherman left the city in ruins when he departed on November 16, 1864.

RICHMOND

This panoramic view of Richmond in 1865 was taken on Belle Isle, the location of another infamous prisoner-of-war camp for Yankee soldiers. Across the James River, the old Capitol of the Confederacy, once again a state house, looms above the city at far left.

FROM BELLE ISLE

Much of Richmond was in ruins at the end of the war. Fires started by the retreating Rebels spread quickly through the area below the Capitol. The fires were eventually controlled by Union troops, who had to blow up buildings to stem the conflagration in what became known as "the burnt district."

THE BURNT DISTRICT

CHAPTER NINE

THE WILDERNESS

In the tangled mass of the Wilderness battlefield, some eighteen months after the battle, photographer
G. O. Brown made this image of battle-damaged trees and the skeletal remains of a fallen soldier.

THE
WILDERNESS

THE BATTLE OF THE WILDERNESS, FOUGHT ON *MAY 5 AND 6, 1864,*

WAS A BLOODY TWO-DAY STALEMATE—

THE FIRST OF MANY EPIC BATTLES BETWEEN **GRANT** AND **LEE** IN VIRGINIA.

The Wilderness is remembered most for

CONFUSED, HORRIFIC COMBAT

in the dense undergrowth and tangled thickets of an area that had been forested years earlier.

The 3-D photographs of the Wilderness in the Robin Stanford collection show just how daunting the battlefield really was. These images, among the rarest that Stanford owns, also reveal new information about this obscure photographic series.

Civil War photohistorian William A. Frassanito says Stanford's Wilderness views "serve as a Rosetta stone" for the series. They identify the photographer as G. O. Brown of Baltimore. They establish that the series was issued commercially. And they date the photos to April 1865, although that date remains problematic.

Much remains to be learned about Brown. He may have been close to Gettysburg photographer Hanson E. Weaver. Stanford's Wilderness views were originally part of a col-

lection owned by Weaver's wife.

Brown apparently visited several battlefields. John Richter, a leading war view collector, has a group, including three of the Wilderness images, that all appear to be Brown views. All have handwritten backmarks with the same handwriting. Other views in Richter's group include scenes of Baltimore, war-torn Richmond, and Fredericksburg.

The trees are without leaves in these images, so they were taken in the fall, winter, or early spring. The original handwritten caption on one of the images says, "View taken April 1865." But Noel G. Harrison, a park historian at Fredericksburg, notes that two of the backmarks refer to a "Cemetery No. 2" and another photo in the series shows Cemetery No. 1. These temporary cemeteries

were not established until June 1865. Thus, the date they were taken cannot be confirmed with the evidence currently available.

The late Wendell W. Lang, Jr., who extensively researched the Wilderness photos, identified sixty different images, including thirty-four stereo views, in the library at West Point. They are part of the collection of Gen. Orlando Poe, the photography enthusiast who brought George Barnard to Nashville and later donated his collection to his alma mater.

Stanford's fifteen Wilderness views give rise to hope that more will be found. The numbers on the backs of her cards range from three to ninety-nine. So there is room, at least in Brown's indexing system, for many additional views.

☆

THE RUINS OF
WILDERNESS TAVERN

Not all of the Wilderness battlefield was dense underbrush. This view shows the foundation of the Wilderness Tavern, which was destroyed, apparently by fire, in 1865. Barely visible in the distance is Ellwood, or the "Lacy House." Robert E. Lee spent the night there in 1863, and three Union generals successively made it their headquarters during the Wilderness battle.

WHAT THE
DEFENDERS SAW

The Wilderness woods in front of the Rebel lines near the Spottswood House looked like this—a dense, tangled mass of young trees and underbrush. This expanse of thicket had replaced the forest, which had been cut years earlier to provide wood for the wooden plank roads in the area, the shafts of nearby gold mines, and local tanneries and iron furnaces.

The caption on this remarkable image, possibly published here for the first time, says, "Hawkins Girls, Who Saw Sights, Wilderness Battlefield." The Hawkins House, however, was closer to the Chancellorsville battlefield, and research by Noel G. Harrison suggests the most dramatic sights these women saw were during that 1863 battle. The Hawkins home was used as a headquarters by Gen. Carl Schurz, who spent the night there on May 1, 1863. The six women, from the Hawkins and Downer families, witnessed the mass confusion that erupted among the Union soldiers camped around the home the next day as the Confederates under Stonewall Jackson swept through the area during their famous flank attack. One Confederate in that attack remembered his brief visit to the Hawkins Farm. " . . . As I passed the dwelling, I saw several ladies who were wildly rejoicing," he wrote.

THE HAWKINS GIRLS

REMAINS OF UNBURIED SOLDIERS

Some of the soldiers who fell in battle remained unburied after the armies departed. When photographer G. O. Brown visited the area after the war, he found some of their remains in the woods one-half mile southeast of the Chancellorsville House.

WHERE WADSWORTH FELL

The same artillery shell that splintered this tree in the Wilderness was said to have struck and killed one of the two horses shot from under Union Gen. James S. Wadsworth, a division commander. Wadsworth fell near here, too, killed by a bullet in the back of the brain during the confused fighting on the second day of the battle on May 6, 1864.

An assistant to photographer G. O. Brown, or perhaps Brown himself, posed at the breastworks of the opposing armies. The top view shows the Rebel works, which were thrown up in the woods and across the Orange Plank Road. The bottom view shows the Union works in the thick of the Wilderness. Many of the small trees show battle damage.

THE OPPOSING
LINES

THE MCCOULL HOUSE

The home of the Neil McCoull family is actually in the heart of the Spotsylvania battlefield. It became the headquarters of Confederate Gen. Richard S. Ewell during the battle of Spotsylvania Court House. On May 10, 1864, after repulsing a nearby Union attack, seven Rebel generals, including Robert E. Lee, gathered at the little house to discuss the events of the day. The home was badly damaged in the battle.

THE FIRST MEMORIAL

This photograph, although labeled "Wilderness field," apparently shows the Spotsylvania battlefield. A road traverses the scene in the distance. The view was said to have been taken near the "triangle of death," an apparent reference to the Bloody Angle. The sign on the tree is likely the battlefield's first memorial. The verse is from Theodore O'Hara's popular Mexican War–era poem, "Bivouac of the Dead."

THREE FALLEN SOLDIERS

In this haunting image, the skulls and bones of three fallen soldiers face skyward in the thick woods of the Wilderness battlefield. G. O. Brown found the remains near the location of Cemetery No. 2, a temporary soldiers' cemetery created in June 1865.

**WHAT WAS LEFT IN
THE WOODS**

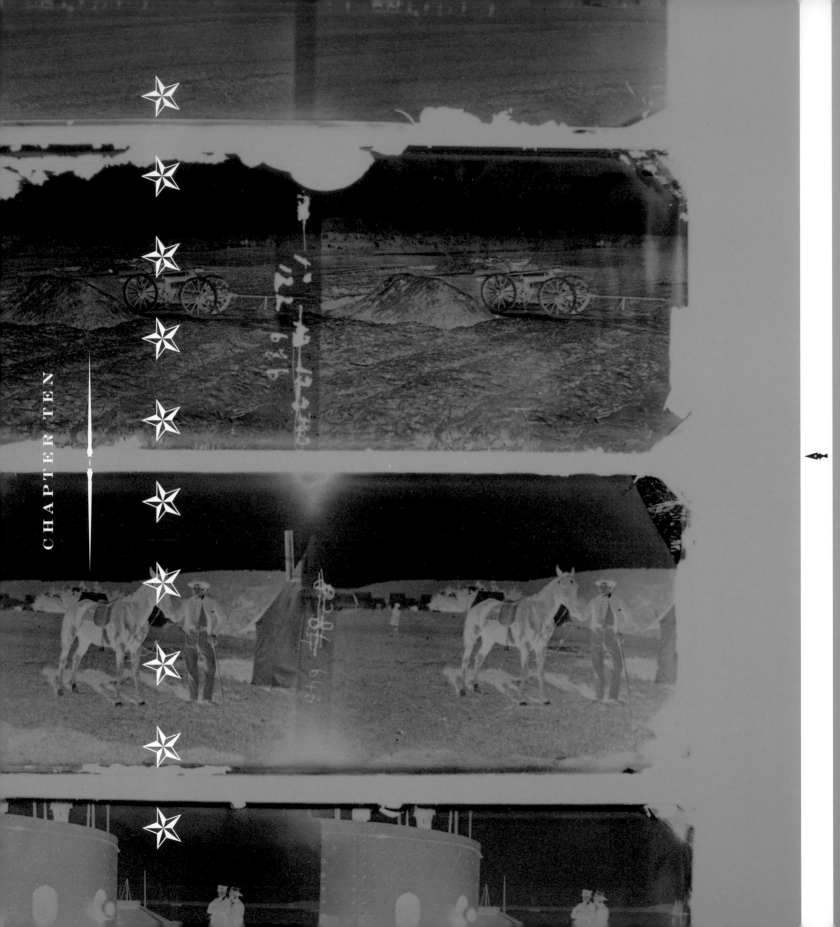

CHAPTER TEN

GLASS PLATE NEGATIVES

(Photograph by Paul Hogroian)

GLASS PLATES

ONE OF THE BEST-KNOWN AND **MOST POIGNANT FABLES** ABOUT
CIVIL WAR PHOTOGRAPHY IS THE STORY ABOUT HOW

THOUSANDS OF ORIGINAL WARTIME GLASS PLATE NEGATIVES
were used as
PANES FOR GREENHOUSE GLASS.

**The great irony in the tale was that the same sun that created the images
soon burned away any trace of them.**

I have never seen any documentation to support this story, so I remain skeptical. Perhaps thousands of common portrait negatives met this fate. But many of the negatives of the most historic photos of the war have survived in some form.

The two largest producers and sellers of war views, by far, were Alexander Gardner and the E. & H.T. Anthony Company. Gardner and his associates produced at least 1,000 and possibly as many as 1,200 stereo views of the war, various records show. The Anthony Company's complete list of war views in its 1869 catalog totals 1,407 stereographs.

Of a potential 2,600 stereo images, the Library of Congress says it has at least one of the halves of the stereo negatives for 2,172 photographs. Some of those 2,172 indexed negatives—perhaps 5 to 10 percent—are broken, missing, or too badly damaged to use. Still, about three-fourths have survived.

The greater loss has been with the full stereoscopic negatives. The Library of Congress lists only 658 intact full stereoscopic negatives. Virtually all of them are Gardner images. The other 1,514 negatives are often only one-half of the original twin-image negatives. In many instances, both halves of the stereo negative exist, but they have been cut and are stored in separate sleeves under the same negative number. Among those for which only one half of the stereo negative remains, there is no record of when or why the original stereoscopic negative was cut, or what happened to the other half.

The images reproduced in this chapter, as well as others scattered elsewhere in the book, are from new contact prints made directly from original glass plate stereoscopic negatives. Normally, prints from the Civil War negatives are made from copy negatives. But the Library of Congress does not have copy negatives of the full stereoscopic glass plates. These new prints have been cropped to show as much of the original scene as possible, and the images have been inverted for proper stereo viewing.

Paul Hogroian, who works for the Library of Congress photoduplication service, made the new prints. "Most of the Civil War negatives print reasonably well," he says. But some have deteriorated even since the half-stereo copy negatives were made twenty or thirty years ago. Hogroian works carefully and reverently when he is making prints directly from glass plates: "It's amazing to work with them, knowing that these are the actual things that were on the battlefield. But I'm always deathly afraid when I'm handling them that I'm going to break one. So far I never have."

☆

AN ANTIETAM FIELD HOSPITAL

Forty-five of seventy-nine 3-D negatives of the Antietam battlefield by Gardner have survived in their complete stereoscopic form, including this one showing the tents of a makeshift field hospital on the Smith farm near the upper bridge. Dr. Anson Hurd of the 14th Indiana Volunteers stands in attendance.

IN CAMP AFTER THE BATTLE

Photohistorian William A. Frassanito has determined that the officer standing in the center of this group portrait of Union officers after the battle of Antietam is Lt. Alonzo Cushing, who died less than a year after this stereograph was made while fighting beside his battery near the copse of trees at Gettysburg during Pickett's Charge. Sitting at left is Evan Thomas, who was killed in ambush by the Modoc Indians a decade later in California.

One of the most unusual of Gardner's Antietam photographs is this one, whose negative survives despite a crack that runs the length of the glass. (The crack does not appear uniform because the images have been inverted for proper 3-D viewing.) The original caption says, "Picnic Party at Antietam Bridge," although it seems inconceivable that anyone would want to picnic at the ghastly, foul-smelling battlefield only five days after the battle.

At the border of North and South along the Potomac River in October 1862, a lone horseman stands in profile before Gardner's camera. In the background, on Maryland soil, is the small village of Berlin (now Brunswick). The Confederates burned the bridge at right in June 1861, prompting the construction by Union forces of the pontoon bridge on the left.

TWO FREDERICKSBURG HOUSES

THE MARYE HOUSE

The Marye House was at the top of Marye's Heights. It was the focal point of the ill-conceived attack by Union Gen. Ambrose Burnside on December 13, 1862 and was the scene of another battle on May 3, 1863. By the time James Gibson took this photograph in May 1864, the yard was full of rifle pits, and the house was thoroughly shot up but still being used as a hospital.

THE PHILLIPS HOUSE

The smoldering ruins of the Phillips House in February 1863 seemed to reflect the disastrous plans made by Burnside inside the dwelling two months earlier when it was his headquarters. The fire apparently was an accident—set by Union soldiers who made a campfire in the attic to keep warm. Union soldiers also fought the blaze.

GETTYSBURG

The emulsion is flaking off this historic negative of the dedication ceremony of the Soldiers' National Cemetery in Gettysburg on November 19, 1863. In *Early Photography at Gettysburg,* author William A. Frassanito established that the negative was produced by Alexander Gardner. The subtle rise in the crowd on the horizon line just right of the center of the image is the location of the speakers' platform, where Lincoln delivered the Gettysburg Address.

THE GETTYSBURG ADDRESS

**A CAVALRY
COMMANDER**

Judson Kilpatrick, an aggressive Union cavalry commander, was known as "Kill-Cavalry" because of his reputation of being rough on his men and their horses. Personally brave, he was also known as a ladies' man and was once forced to flee his camp with a female companion—but without his pants—during a surprise Confederate cavalry assault. He recovered to rally his men and fight back.

**THE CUMBERLAND
LANDING PANORAMA**

This is the right view of a three-image panorama, by photographer James Gibson, of the Union encampment at Cumberland Landing on the Pamunkey River in May 1862. The center view shows the landing. The left view, which shows the main camp, is published on page 95 of *The Civil War in Depth*.

Inside hastily constructed Harewood Hospital in Washington, D.C., the sick and wounded peer at the camera in a view apparently taken in the summer of 1864. Mosquito nets sit above each bed, ready to be pulled down at night to protect against the pests, which were ever-present in the capital during the hot months.

HAREWOOD HOSPITAL

CHAPTER ELEVEN

PETERSBURG GAS WORKS

The photographic wagon used by photographer Timothy O'Sullivan, who took this image,
sits by the heavily damaged Petersburg Gas Works in May 1865.

THE LOOK *of* WAR

The period from 1860 to 1920
WAS THE ERA OF THE STEREOGRAPH IN AMERICAN CULTURE.

THE CIVIL WAR, WHICH CAME AT THE BEGINNING OF THAT SIXTY-YEAR SPAN, MAY HAVE BEEN BETTER

DOCUMENTED BY THE STEREOSCOPIC CAMERA THAN ANY OTHER MOMENTOUS EVENT OF THAT TIME.

Perhaps it was because so much happened over the four years of the war. Maybe it was due in part to the fact that the craft of stereo photography was still young and the photographers and the companies they worked for had not yet adopted some of the habits and conventions that limited the scope of their work in later years.

In any event, the stereo camera has given us a remarkable range of 3-D views of the Civil War. The twin-lens camera revealed gruesome scenes, like the mangled corpses at Antietam and Gettysburg. It preserved historic moments, such as Lincoln's inaugurations and his battlefield visit at Antietam. And it captured the scenic images that stereo photography is so well known for, such as

Lulu Falls on Lookout Mountain. It even captured, at Fort Sumter in 1863, the first photographs of combat action taken while the photographer was under fire.

One reason the war was so well documented in 3-D photos is the number of events that happened in reasonably close proximity to urban centers. In the North, photographers became part of the army. They sometimes provided a service—map reproduction—and usually became friends with the top officers, thereby gaining access to the sights and scenes on the battlefield that could lead to commercially profitable stereographs.

Time and time again, their cameras focused on scenes that remind us of the cost of war. It is one thing to know that more than a

half million soldiers, North and South, were killed or wounded in battle. It is quite another experience to see the rigid expressions of death on some of those men as preserved by the photographs of the Civil War.

The work of the Civil War photographers set a standard for American war photojournalism that was, arguably, unmatched until World War II. And it established a historic record of the war in photographs—one that continues to grow each year as remarkable new images come to light.

☆

Graves, of the Six Men hung at Andersonville, Ga. July 11th 1864.

JUSTICE FOR HUMAN PREDATORS

In the squalor and degradation of Andersonville Prison in Georgia, some Northern prisoners formed gangs that preyed on fellow prisoners. The worst of the hoodlums were tried by their comrades. Some were forced to run a brutal gauntlet. Six were hanged. The third grave from the right belongs to Willie Collins, whose rope broke on the drop. Already nearly strangled, a gasping Collins was strung up again.

A BUSY BURYING GROUND

The Hollywood Cemetery, Richmond's main cemetery, was a sad and busy place during the war. A surplus of death and a shortage of supplies meant that most of the dead had to be laid to rest with only simple wooden headboards marking their graves.

Entered according to Act of Congress in the year 1862, by Alex. Gardner, in the Clerk's Office of the District Court of the District of Columbia.

The photographs of the dead at Antietam by Alexander Gardner were riveting to those who saw them. These Confederates fell on the west side of Hagerstown Pike just north of Sharpsburg. The 3-D views sold for 50 cents each— more than twice the cost of an average non-war view—and apparently still sold quite well. The success of the Antietam series prompted Gardner to move quickly at Gettysburg, where he succeeded in photographing more unburied casualties.

On May 20, 1864, the day after the last engagement at Spotsylvania, photographer Timothy O'Sullivan, who had been with Gardner at Gettysburg, photographed war casualties on his own for the first time, although he was still working for Gardner. This Confederate, with a "prop" rifle laid across his body, fell in the battle around Alsop's Farm.

1861   The War For the Union.   1865   1861   Photographic War History.   1865

725.   Confederate Dead on the Battlefield.
[OR DESCRIPTION OF THIS VIEW SEE THE OTHER SIDE OF THIS CARD.]

PHOTOGRAPHIC HISTORY

THE WAR FOR THE UNION

Entered according to Act of Congress in the year 1865, by E & H T Anthony & Co., in the Clerk's Office of District Court of U.S. for the So. District of New York.

TRENCH WARFARE

This dramatic 3-D view looks as if it could have been taken on the front lines of Europe in World War I. But this is the Confederate Fort Mahone outside Petersburg, Virginia, after it fell to the Union army in early April 1865.

A NORTHERN CITY IN RUINS

On July 30, 1864, the Rebels torched Chambersburg, Pennsylvania, shown here in ruins. Four hundred buildings burned. Early that same morning, the Federals blew up a section of the Confederate defensive lines outside Petersburg, but lost the battle in the crater made by the explosion.

The grieving masses crowd around the burial vault for Abraham Lincoln at Oak Ridge Cemetery in Springfield, Illinois, on May 4, 1865. Umbrellas are raised not against the rain but to ward off the rays of the sun on an oppressively hot spring day. Lincoln was assassinated five days after Lee surrendered at Appomattox.

THE DAY LINCOLN WAS BURIED

RESOURCE GUIDE

The Work of William A. Frassanito

Photohistorian William A. Frassanito was the first to use Civil War photographs not only as illustrations but as tools for scholarly historical research. In the process he has published dozens of previously unpublished Civil War photographs, located the precise spots where many images were taken, and unearthed a treasure trove of information about the battlefields and scenes they show. All of his work, thankfully, remains in print by Thomas Publications, P.O. Box 3031, Gettysburg, Pennsylvania 17325. His major works are: *Gettysburg: A Journey in Time* (1975); *Antietam: The Photographic Legacy of America's Bloodiest Day* (1978); *Grant and Lee: The Virginia Campaigns 1864–1865* (1983); *Early Photography at Gettysburg* (1995); *Gettysburg Then and Now* (1996); and the *Gettysburg Then and Now Companion* (1997).

More Books

★ MARY PANZER, the curator of photographs at the Smithsonian National Portrait Gallery, has written the definitive study on M. B. Brady and his work: *Mathew Brady and the Image of History,* published in 1997 by the Smithsonian Institution Press, Washington, D.C.

★ HARVEY TEAL's new comprehensive history of early photography in South Carolina is *Partners With the Sun, South Carolina Photographers and Their Photography, 1840–1940.* It was published by the University of South Carolina Press in May 2000.

★ D. MARK KATZ's biography of Alexander Gardner, the lavish *Witness to an Era: The Life and Photographs of Alexander Gardner,* was reprinted in April 1999 by Rutledge Hill Press, Nashville, Tennessee.

For more information on stereo views in general, consult *Stereo Views: An Illustrated History and Price Guide,* by John Waldsmith. Radnor, Pennsylvania: Wallace-Homestead Book Company, 1991.

Buying Original Views

There are a number of Internet sources for original stereo views of the Civil War. The eBay auction site (www.ebay.com) usually has several Civil War stereo views for sale at all times under Collectibles: Photographs: Stereoviews. Civil War dealer Len Rosa also usually has a selection of war views on his Web site (www.warbetweenthestates.com). Antique photography dealer Jeffrey Kraus (www.mhv.net/~jkraus/) also sells war views. And stereoview auctioneer John Saddy has regular auctions that usually include some war views (www3.sympatico.ca/john.saddy.3d/). For a spectacular look at early American photography in general, visit the first fully online photography museum, Wm. B. Becker's American Museum of Photography (www.photographymuseum.com). For more information on the photography of the Civil War, visit www.civilwarphotography.com.

Gibson's Photographic Gallery

To see how Civil War wet-plate photography was really done, visit photographer Rob Gibson at Gibson's Photographic Gallery, 65 Steinwehr Avenue, Gettysburg, Pennsylvania. Gibson operates the only nineteenth-century style photographic studio in Gettysburg. There are also several shops in Gettysburg that sell original war views and other Civil War antiques, including Sword and Saber, The Horse Soldier, Fields of Glory, and the Gettysburg Antique Center.

The National Stereoscopic Association

The National Stereoscopic Association (NSA) is a nonprofit organization that encourages and promotes the study and collection of stereoscopic images. It publishes *Stereo World* six times a year and conducts an annual convention with a trade fair and auction. For membership information, write the association at P.O. Box 14801, Columbus, Ohio 43214.

Replacement Viewers

If the stereo viewer for this book is missing, contact:

American Paper Optics, Inc.
3080 Bartlett Corporate Drive
Bartlett, TN 38133

Phone: (901) 381-1515
Fax: (901) 381-1517
Web Site: www.3dglassesonline.com

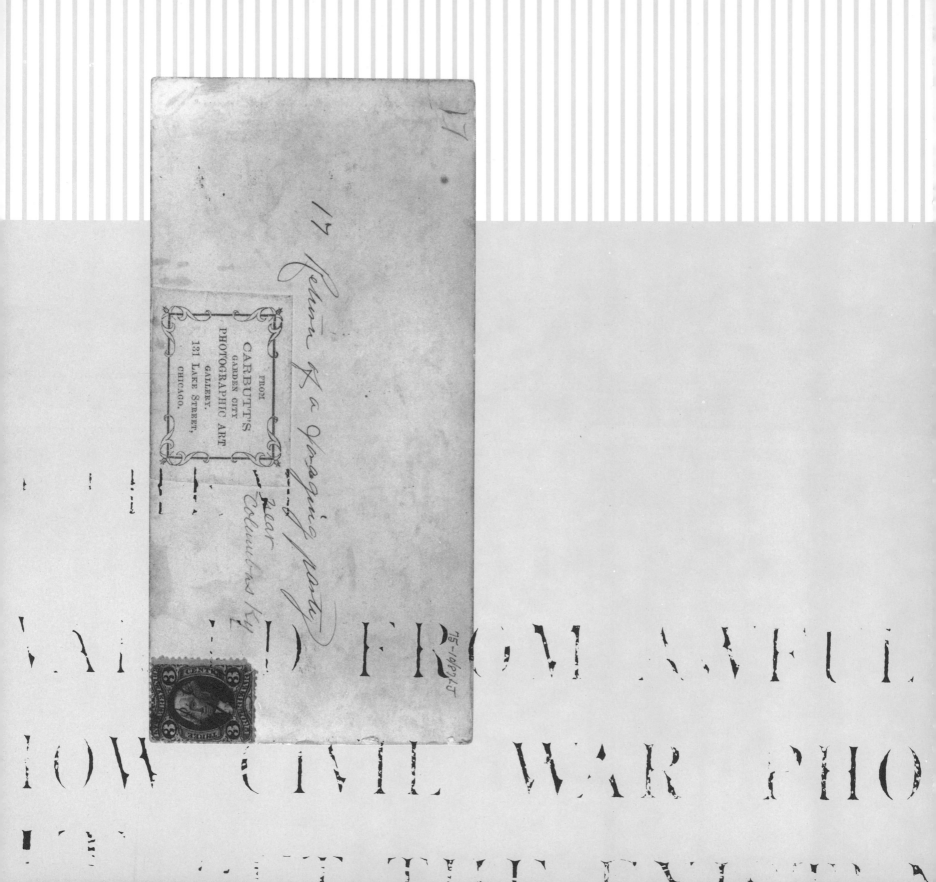